AFTER 20 MINUTES UNITED WERE EIGHT GOALS DOWN TO ARCH RIVALS GRIMTHORPE

OH NO! IN GOES NUMBER NINE

IT'S A DISASTEROUS DEBUT FOR THE NEW FISH KEEPER

WHAT A LOAD OF RUBBISH!

BOO!!

IN THE FULCHESTER DUG OUT...

WELL TOMMY, NINE DOWN ALREADY THANKS TO THE YOUNG FISH LAD

THIS IS HIS FIRST AND LAST GAME FOR UNITED!

HAVING KIDNAPPED THEIR FISH-LIKE KEEPER AND REPLACED HIM WITH AN INFLATABLE REPLICA, GRIMTHORPE CITY BOSS GUS PARKER WAS EXPECTING AN EASY WIN OVER FULCHESTER UNITED...

CD SD 9.84

BUT NEARBY, IN A WINDOW OVERLOOKING THE GROUND...

TIME TO SAY YOUR PRAYERS THOMSON! THIS IS THE LAST GAME BILLY THE FISH WILL EVER PLAY!

BANG!

HEY! WHERE'S THE KEEPER?

UH?

POP! THE NEW 'FISH LIKE' NUMBER ONE SEEMS TO HAVE EXPLODED!

THOMSON HAS JUST VANISHED INTO THIN AIR!

NOT QUITE...

THIS TATTERED BALLOON IS A CLUE. THE FISH TYPE GOALIE MUST HAVE BEEN KIDNAPPED AND REPLACED BY A LIFE-LIKE INFLATABLE REPLICA!

BUT WHOEVER BURST THE BALLOON WASN'T TO KNOW THAT

INDEED OFFICER. SOMEONE IS OUT TO MURDER THE BRILLIANT FISH KEEPER! BUT WHO?

AFTER THE MATCH, UNITED COACH SYD PRESTON WAS TIDYING UP WHEN...

FUNNY! TERRY JACKSON HAS LEFT HIS LOCKER OPEN

WHAT THE ?!?

THIS IS. ODD...

WHAT WOULD JACKSON, OUR UNSETTLED RESERVE TEAM KEEPER WANT WITH A HIGH POWERED RIFLE?

MEANWHILE GUS PARKER AND A VICTORIOUS GRIMTHORPE SIDE HAD RETURNED TO THEIR TRAINING CAMP WHERE THE REAL BILLY THOMSON REMAINED A HELPLESS KIDNAP VICTIM...

FOURTEEN NIL, EH BOSS? A GOOD RESULT. PITTY ABOUT THE INFLATABLE KEEPER BURSTING.

ONLY A MINOR SETBACK TO MY WICKED PLANS, WILF.

NOW THAT UNITED WILL BE LOOKING FOR THEIR MISSING STAR, WE WILL HAVE TO HIDE HIM SOMEWHERE. A PLACE THEY WOULD NEVER THINK OF LOOKING... RIGHT IN THE MIDDLE OF THE GRIMTHORPE CITY GOAL!

YOU WON'T GET AWAY WITH IT, PARKER. I'LL NEVER PLAY FOR GRIMTHORPE CITY! NEVER!!

MAY I INTRODUCE MR. ROMANO, A DISCREDITED HYPNOTIST. NO DOUBT HE WILL SOON CHANGE YOUR MIND!

GOOD THINKING, BOSS

YOU FEEL TIRED. YOU ARE FALLING ASLEEP.

WITH A GRIMTHORPE CITY STRIP SUSPENDED FROM THIS SPECIALLY ADJUSTED COAT HANGER BILLY THOMSON WILL BE UN-NOTICED IN OUR GOAL! AND WE WILL BE UNBEATABLE.!!

IS BILLY SET TO PLAY FOR GRIMTHORPE UNDER ROMANO'S EVIL SPELL? HAS HE PLAYED HIS LAST GAME FOR UNITED? AND WHO IS OUT TO MURDER BILLY THE FISH? FIND OUT IN THE NEXT EPISODE...

THE OFFICIAL 'ALL OLD'

VIZ
BILLY the FISH
FOOTBALL YEARBOOK

**The entire Billy the Fish story to date.
Originally published in Viz issues 10 to 44,
1983 to 1990.**

Written and illustrated by
Chris Donald, Simon Thorp and Graham Dury.
Additional material by Simon Donald.

Fulchester United are sponsored by **Go! Discs.**

ISBN 1 870 870 16 6

Published in Great Britain by John Brown Publishing Limited,
The Boathouse, Crabtree Lane, Fulham, London SW6 8NJ.

First printing November 1990.

Copyright © by House of Viz/John Brown Publishing Limited.
All rights reserved. No part of this publication may be reproduced
or transmitted in any form or by any means, electronic or
mechanical, including photocopy, recording, Pantograph, potato print
or any information storage or retrieval system now known or to be
invented, without permission in writing from the Publisher.

Printed and bound in Great Britain.

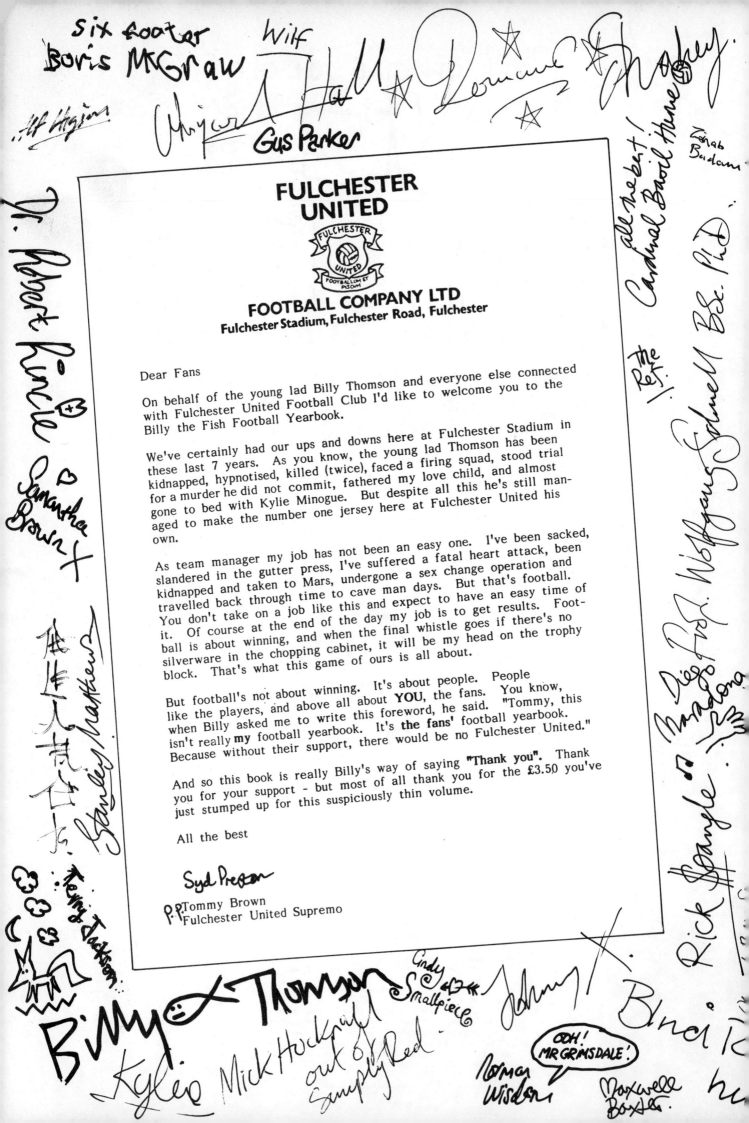

FULCHESTER UNITED

FOOTBALL COMPANY LTD
Fulchester Stadium, Fulchester Road, Fulchester

Dear Fans

On behalf of the young lad Billy Thomson and everyone else connected with Fulchester United Football Club I'd like to welcome you to the Billy the Fish Football Yearbook.

We've certainly had our ups and downs here at Fulchester Stadium in these last 7 years. As you know, the young lad Thomson has been kidnapped, hypnotised, killed (twice), faced a firing squad, stood trial for a murder he did not commit, fathered my love child, and almost gone to bed with Kylie Minogue. But despite all this he's still managed to make the number one jersey here at Fulchester United his own.

As team manager my job has not been an easy one. I've been sacked, slandered in the gutter press, I've suffered a fatal heart attack, been kidnapped and taken to Mars, undergone a sex change operation and travelled back through time to cave man days. But that's football. You don't take on a job like this and expect to have an easy time of it. Of course at the end of the day my job is to get results. Football is about winning, and when the final whistle goes if there's no silverware in the chopping cabinet, it will be my head on the trophy block. That's what this game of ours is all about.

But football's not about winning. It's about people. People like the players, and above all about **YOU**, the fans. You know, when Billy asked me to write this foreword, he said. "Tommy, this isn't really **my** football yearbook. It's **the fans'** football yearbook. Because without their support, there would be no Fulchester United."

And so this book is really Billy's way of saying **"Thank you"**. Thank you for your support - but most of all thank you for the £3.50 you've just stumped up for this suspiciously thin volume.

All the best

Syd Preston

p.p. Tommy Brown
Fulchester United Supremo

BILLY the FISH

BORN HALF MAN, HALF FISH, FULCHESTER'S BRILLIANT YOUNG KEEPER 'BILLY THOMSON' HAD AN UNCANNY ABILITY TO SWIM THROUGH THE AIR. UNDERGOING HYPNOSIS IN THE HANDS OF ARCH RIVALS GRIMTHORPE CITY, THE FISH-LIKE WONDER WAS UNAWARE OF AN ATTEMPT HAVING BEEN MADE ON HIS LIFE.

CD 5-85

MEANWHILE FULCHESTER BOSS TOMMY BROWN HAD NO CHOICE BUT TO SELECT HIS UNSETTLED RESERVE KEEPER TERRY JACKSON FOR UNITED'S VITAL CUP CLASH WITH MUCH FANCIED ROSSDALE ROVERS...

BUT WITH THE GAME ONLY SECONDS OLD

TERRY JACKSON, I ARREST YOU FOR THE ATTEMPTED MURDER OF BILLY THE FISH

BUT... BUT...

IT LOOKS LIKE AN EARLY SHOWER FOR THE FULCHESTER Nº1

THIS HIGH POWERED RIFLE WAS FOUND IN YOUR LOCKER. YOU'D BETTER COME WITH US.

BUT EVEN AS JACKSON WAS BEING LEAD AWAY...

MY BALL!!

CRIKEY! AN EXPLODING BALL!

BOOM!!

YES, AND IT LOOKS LIKE CURTAINS FOR THE ROSSDALE SKIPPER!

BUT WAIT A MOMENT! THE KAPUT CAPTAIN IS A ROBOT!!

OUR KEEPER ARRESTED, THE BALL EXPLODES AND THE ROSSDALE SKIPPER EXPOSED AS A ROBOT! THIS IS JUST THE KIND OF START WE DIDN'T NEED!

MMM, BUT WITH EIGHTY MINUTES TO PLAY THE GAME COULD STILL GO EITHER WAY

BUT AS AN ANXIOUS TOMMY BROWN LOOKED ON, FULCHESTER LEGS BEGAN TO TIRE

UH! MY LEGS ARE SO TIRED

HA! TOO SLOW! I'LL TAKE THAT

...AND ROSSDALE BEGAN TO TAKE ADVANTAGE

HAH! NO KEEPER TO BEAT AND A DEFENCE BARELY ABLE TO STAND. I CAN'T BELIEVE MY LUCK

BOO! ANOTHER TAP IN GOAL FOR ROSSDALE

UGGH!!

BY HALF-TIME FULCHESTER HAD ALMOST COME TO A STANDSTILL

TWELVE-NIL DOWN AT THE INTERVAL! A DISAPPOINTING FORTY-FIVE MINUTES FOR UNITED!

YEAH! THEY'LL HAVE TO PULL THEIR SOCKS UP IN THE SECOND PERIOD

IN THE DRESSING ROOM

HEY! WHAT'S THIS IN MY BOOT?

THERE'S SOMETHING IN MINE TOO

NO WONDER YOUR LEGS TIRED! THERE ARE LEAD WEIGHTS IN THESE BOOTS!!

HEY! YEAH!

AND MINE TOO!

AND MINE!

THESE DIDN'T GET HERE BY ACCIDENT!

SOMEONE IS OUT TO MAKE TROUBLE FOR FULCHESTER UNITED. THE QUESTION IS WHO?

HOPEFULLY THIS TEA WILL REVIVE A FEW TIRED LEGS IN TIME FOR THE NEXT ALL IMPORTANT FORTY-FIVE MINUTES

THIS TEA TASTES A BIT STRANGE

YEAH! IT'S A TRIFLE PECULIAR!

STRANGE, IT'S NOT LIKE OLD ALF HIGSON, THE BOOT CLEANER FULCHESTER REJECTED AS AN APPRENTICE FORTY YEARS AGO, TO MAKE THE TEA!

MEANWHILE AT THE GRIMTHORPE TRAINING CAMP DISCREDITED HYPNOTIST ROMANO HAS BAD NEWS FOR EVIL TEAM BOSS GUS PARKER...

I'M AFRAID I HAVE BAD NEWS FOR YOU MR. PARKER

MY HYPNOSIS HAS PROVED TOO MUCH FOR THE CAPTIVE YOUNG FISH KEEPER. BILLY THOMSON IS DEAD!!!

WHO IS BEHIND THE STRANGE OCCURENCES AT FULCHESTER STADIUM? IS BILLY THE FISH DEAD? AND ARE UNITED SET FOR AN EARLY CUP EXIT?

FIND OUT IN THE NEXT ISSUE

BILLY the FISH

BORN HALF MAN, HALF FISH, UNITED'S BRILLIANT YOUNG KEEPER BILLY THOMSON HAD BEEN TAKEN PRISONER BY GUS PARKER, EVIL TEAM BOSS OF ARCH RIVALS GRIMTHORPE CITY...

CD 8.85

WITHOUT THE MISSING 'FISH BOY' WONDER AND AMIDST UNUSUAL OCCURENCES AT FULCHESTER STADIUM A DISAPPOINTING UNITED SIDE HAD SLUMPED TO TWELVE-'NIL DOWN BY HALF-TIME IN THEIR ALL IMPORTANT CUP CLASH WITH MUCH FANCIED ROSSDALE ROVERS...

MEANWHILE AT THE GRIMTHORPE TRAINING CAMP GUS PARKER HAS JUST LEARNT OF THOMSON'S DEATH UNDER HYPNOSIS.

DID YOU BURY THE FISH KID LIKE I TOLD YOU, WILF?

YEAH BOSS. IT'LL BE A REAL NICE SURPRISE FOR TOMMY BROWN!

HA HA HA HA HA HA HA HA HA !!!

MEANWHILE AT FULCHESTER STADIUM

ODD! THE ENTIRE TEAM HAVE FALLEN ASLEEP AND THE GAME RE-STARTS IN 2 MINUTES!

ZZZZZZ...

WE'LL NEVER REVERSE A TWELVE GOAL DEFECIT WITH OUR TEAM OUT FOR THE COUNT!

DON'T WORRY. I'D SUSPECTED THAT THE HALF-TIME TEA WOULD BE DRUGGED SO I HIRED A TEAM OF ACTORS TO IMPERSONATE FULCHESTER IN THE FIRST HALF

GOOD THINKING BOSS

THE REAL FULCHESTER TEAM ARE IN HERE, WIDE AWAKE AND READY FOR THE SECOND HALF.

TERRIFIC!

PRIVATE

WE'VE STILL GOT EVERYTHING TO PLAY FOR IN THE SECOND PERIOD

BUT AS THE SECOND HALF GOT UNDERWAY...

UNGH! I'VE TRIPPED ON SOMETHING

THE FULCHESTER FORWARD HAS BEEN UPENDED!

PENALTY!?!

IT APPEARS TO BE A GRAVESTONE

I'M AFRAID OUR BRILLIANT FISH LIKE KEEPER IS DEAD, AND BURIED HERE... ON THE EDGE OF THE 18 YARD AREA!

R.I.P BILLY the FISH

NO DOUBT THIS IS THE WORK OF GUS PARKER

WITH THE YOUNG FISH BOY DEAD WE'LL HAVE TO THROW EVERYTHING INTO ATTACK. IF ONLY WE HAD A STRIKER ON THE BENCH

ISN'T OLD REX FINDLAY STILL REGISTERED AS A PLAYER?

HMM! PEANUT SELLER REX MAY BE BLIND BUT HE COULD BE OUR ONLY CHANCE!

THE 64 YEAR OLD VETERAN COMES ON WITH TEN MINUTES LEFT TO PLAY

3

HEY LOOK EVERYONE. IT'S OLD REX FINDLAY

HE'S PUT ON HIS BOOTS FOR THE FIRST TIME IN 25 YEARS!

HAHA! UNITED MUST BE REALLY DESPERATE

IMMEDIATELY THE BLIND VETERAN IS IN THE ACTION

OLD FINDLAY BEAT 3 MEN!

GOAL!!! TWELVE-ONE

UNITED ARE BACK IN THE GAME

NOT BAD FOR A BLIND MAN!!

AND THE GOALS KEPT COMING...

IT'S THERE!

FINDLAY MUST HAVE 'BAT LIKE' VISION!!

WHAT A GOAL!!

AT 64 FINDLAY HAS LOST NONE OF HIS APPETITE FOR THE GAME

SOON

GOAL!!!

GOAL Nº11 FOR THE AGEING FRONT MAN

ONE MORE AND WE'RE LEVEL!

IN THE FINAL MINUTE AS UNITED PUSH FORWARD

FOUL!!

PENALTY!!

YES! IT'S A SPOT KICK TO UNITED!

STOP THE GAME! I AM RUTHLESS MILLIONAIRE MAXWELL BAXTER. I HAVE JUST BOUGHT FULCHESTER STADIUM AND INTEND TO BUILD A SUPERMARKET. DEMOLITION WILL BEGIN AT ONCE!

IS BILLY THE FISH REALLY DEAD?

CAN BLIND REX FINDLAY COMPLETE HIS QUADRUPLE HATRICK AND SAVE THE GAME FOR UNITED?

OR WILL RUTHLESS MAXWELL BAXTER DEMOLISH THE STADIUM, AND WITH IT THE CLUB?

SEE NEXT ISSUE

BILLY the FISH

HALF MAN, HALF FISH FULCHESTER'S BRILLIANT KEEPER BILLY THOMSON HAD BEEN MURDERED BY EVIL GUS PARKER, BOSS OF NIEGHBOURING GRIMTHORPE CITY. HOWEVER, AIDED BY THEIR BLIND VETERAN STRIKER REX FINDLAY, UNITED HAD FOUGHT BACK TO ONLY 11-12 DOWN IN THEIR VITAL CUP CLASH WITH MUCH FANCIED ROSSDALE.

AWARDED A PENALTY IN THE FINAL MINUTE OF THE GAME, FULCHESTER HAD LOOKED SET TO LEVEL THE SCORES UNTIL RUTHLESS MILLIONAIRE MAXWELL BAXTER INTERVENED...

I AM THE NEW OWNER OF FULCHESTER STADIUM. STOP THIS GAME AT ONCE

WAIT A MOMENT! THIS ISN'T A REAL MILLIONAIRE. IT'S A CARDBOARD REPLICA WITH A HIDDEN TAPE RECORDER!

OKAY THEN LADS, LET'S FINISH THE GAME

PENALTY TO FULCHESTER...

FORWARD STEPS FINDLAY TO COMPLETE HIS QUADRUPLE HATRICK

THIS KICK TO SAVE THE GAME. THE PRESSURE IS CERTAINLY ON!

HA! THAT EFFORT DOESN'T CAUSE ME ANY PROBLEMS. HE'S SHOT IN THE WRONG DIRECTION!

FINDLAY MUST BE MAD. HE'S AIMING AT THE FLOODLIGHTS!

A DISSAPOINTING EFFORT FROM FINDLAY. THE 64-YEAR OLD HAS BLASTED HIS SPOT KICK HOPELESSLY WIDE

HMM! A CUP EXIT NOW LOOKS INEVITABLE FOR US, EH BOSS?

BUT HIGH ABOVE FULCHESTER STADIUM...

HEY LOOK! THE BALL IS BEGINING TO TURN

SMOKE TABS DRINK BEER

IT'S BENDING THROUGH THE AIR LIKE A BOOMERANG!

HOW ABOUT THIS FOR A BANANA SHOT?

WHAT THE..!

GOAL!

IT'S CIRCLED THE GROUND TWICE BEFORE FINDING THE TOP CORNER OF THE NET!

THAT PUTS UNITED LEVEL!

BUY PETROL

AS THE FINAL WHISTLE BLEW

NO WONDER THEY CALLED HIM 'BANANA BOOTS' FINDLAY IN HIS HEYDAY, EH BOSS?

YES. AND HE'S STILL THE MAN TO WATCH IN A DEAD BALL SITUATION

AND IN THE DRESSING ROOM

GREAT GOAL REX. BUT HOW DID YOU MANAGE IT?

TO BE QUITE HONEST TOMMY, I HAD A LITTLE HELP.

THIS IS NO ORDINARY BALL. IT'S A HIGHLY ADVANCED MICRO-AIRCRAFT, DRIVEN BY A TINY JET ENGINE, AND CONTROLLED FROM INSIDE!

MMM! BUT HOW DID YOU FIND A PILOT SMALL ENOUGH TO FIT INSIDE THE BALL?

THERE'S ONLY ONE ANSWER

BILLY THE FISH!!

YES. I'M ALIVE AND WELL. MY FISH-LIKE BODY MADE ME THE OBVIOUS CHOICE TO FLY REX'S JET POWERED AIRCRAFT BALL

BUT... HOLD IT RIGHT THERE.. I AM THE **REAL** MAXWELL BAXTER, CHAIRMAN OF THE LEAGUE COMMITTEE. I ACCUSE YOU OF CHEATING. I HEREBY EXPELL FULCHESTER UNITED FROM THE FOOTBALL LEAGUE

ARE FULCHESTER FINISHED IN THE LEAGUE? SEE THE NEXT ISSUE

BILLY the FISH

BORN HALF MAN, HALF FISH, YOUNG BILLY THOMSON WAS ALL SET TO MAKE THE N°1 JERSEY AT FULCHESTER UNITED HIS OWN UNTIL HE WAS KIDNAPPED BY ARCH RIVALS GRIMTHORPE CITY. MURDERED BY CITY'S EVIL BOSS GUS PARKER, THOMSON SOMEHOW MIRACULOUSLY RECOVERED AND HELPED FULCHESTER TO A DRAW IN THEIR VITAL CUP CLASH WITH MUCH FANCIED ROSSDALE ROVERS.

BUT LEAGUE CHAIRMAN MAXWELL BAXTER HAS ACCUSED UNITED OF FOUL PLAY AND IS ABOUT TO EXPELL TOMMY BROWN'S SIDE FROM THE FOOTBALL LEAGUE...

I HEREBY... I HEREBY EXPELL... I HEREBY... I HEREBY EXPELL...

THIS ISN'T THE **REAL** MAXWELL BAXTER!

IT'S JUST **ANOTHER** CARDBOARD REPLICA!

WITH A HIDDEN TAPE RECORDER

INDEED, BUT THIS LIFE-LIKE DUMMY DIDN'T GET HERE ON ITS OWN. SOMEONE *INSIDE* THIS CLUB MUST BE RESPONSIBLE

NEXT MORNING IN MANAGER TOMMY BROWN'S OFFICE...

YOU WANTED TO SEE ME BOSS?

YES SYD. THERE'S SOMEONE I'D LIKE YOU TO MEET – A **NEW SIGNING** I MADE THIS MORNING

HE'S THE **MYSTERY PLAYER**. FOR THE MOMENT HIS IDENTITY WILL REMAIN A CLOSELY GUARDED SECRET

GREAT IDEA, BOSS. THIS COULD BE JUST THE BOOST OUR SIDE NEEDS IN TIME FOR TOMORROW'S VITAL CUP REPLAY AT ROSSDALE ROAD

WE'VE AGREED A FEE OF AROUND £500,000. YOU GO TO THE SAFE AND FETCH THE MONEY WHILE I TIE UP THE FINAL LOOSE ENDS

OKAY BOSS

BUT AS COACH SYD PRESTON COUNTS OUT THE MONEY...

WE MUST HAVE HAD A GOOD CROWD IN ON SATURDAY

UH? THE LIGHTS...

BAM!

ARRGH!!!

SECONDS LATER...

OH NO! COACH SYD PRESTON HAS BEEN SHOT, AND THE MONEY STOLEN!

WITHIN MINUTES AN AMBULANCE ARRIVES TO RUSH THE *LUCK-LESS* COACH TO HOSPITAL

IS IT SERIOUS? WILL HE PULL THROUGH?

HE'S BADLY INJURED MR. BROWN, BUT HE SHOULD BE FIT IN TIME FOR TOMORROW'S VITAL REPLAY

THE NEXT DAY THE UNITED TEAM ARE ALL SET FOR THE LONG TRIP TO ROSSDALE

YOU'RE LATE, GREEN

SORRY BOSS. I HAD TO GO TO THE GARAGE TO PICK UP MY NEW CAR!

THAT'S ODD. IT'S NOT LIKE QUIET MIDFIELDER TOMMY GREEN TO BE SPLASHING OUT MONEY ON A NEW CAR!

BY 7.15 THAT EVENING FULCHESTER WERE READY TO FACE ROSSDALE IN THE VITAL CUP REPLAY.

I'M SURE THIS CHANGING ROOM LOOKS FAMILIAR

YES. I SEEM TO RECOGNISE IT FROM SOMEWHERE.

QUIET PLEASE LADS. BEFORE YOU GO OUT THERE I THINK IT'S TIME I INTRODUCED YOU ALL TO OUR MYSTERY SIGNING...

MAY I INTRODUCE FULCHESTER'S NEW CENTRE FORWARD...**SHAKIN' STEVENS!**

GOSH! SHAKY... I'VE GOT ALL YOUR RECORDS. WELCOME TO THE TEAM!

AND SO IT WAS A FULCHESTER SIDE BRIMMING WITH CONFIDENCE THAT EMMERGED FROM THE TUNNEL

HEY! WHERE'S THE CROWD?

THE GROUND IS **EMPTY!**

WHERE ARE ROSSDALE?

I KNEW I'D SEEN THIS PLACE BEFORE. THIS IS OUR OWN GROUND – FULCHESTER STADIUM !!

SOMEONE MUST HAVE MOVED THE ROAD SIGNS, LEADING US ROUND IN CIRCLES! NOW WE'RE 200 MILES FROM ROSSDALE, AND THE GAME IS DUE TO KICK-OFF IN LESS THAN TEN MINUTES!!

WILL UNITED REACH ROSSDALE IN TIME? WILL SHAKIN' STEVENS IMPRESS ON HIS FULCHESTER DEBUT? *DON'T MISS THE NEXT ISSUE!*

Born half man, half fish, Fulchester's brilliant young keeper Billy Thomson's uncanny ability had earned his side a draw in their vital cup clash with much fancied Rossdale Rovers. With £500,000 signing Shakin' Stevens set to make his debut United were confident of victory as they set off for the replay at Rossdale Road. But vital road signs along the way had been switched, and with only seconds remaining till kick-off United found themselves in their own Fulchester Stadium, 200 miles from Rossdale!

HOW SERIOUS IS SHAKY'S INJURY? AND WILL JUSTICE BE DONE, OR ARE UNITED REALLY OUT OF THE CUP?   DON'T MISS THE NEXT ISSUE !!!

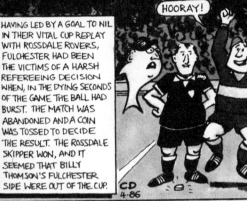

IT LOOKS LIKE SOME KIND OF SPACESHIP, TOMMY.

WELL WHATEVER IT IS WE'RE NEVER GOING TO SHIFT IT IN TIME FOR A TRAINING SESSION THIS AFTERNOON!

BUT IN THE DIRECTOR'S BOX HIGH ABOVE THE GROUND MILLIONAIRE POP STAR CHAIRMAN RICK SPANGLE LOOKED ON WITH INTEREST.

HA HA HA! THAT IS THE LEAST OF YOUR WORRIES! BECAUSE BILLY THOMSON HAS PLAYED HIS LAST GAME FOR FULCHESTER UNITED!!

HIS NEXT GAME WILL NOT BE ON EARTH!

IT WILL BE MILLIONS OF MILES AWAY, AND IN THE RED SHIRT OF DYNAMO MARS!

MEANWHILE AT GRIMTHORPE CITY EVIL BOSS GUS PARKER IS PLANNING A EUROPEAN BREAK FOR HIS PLAYERS...

IS THAT EVERYTHING, WILF?

YEAH, I'VE GOT THE PLANE TICKETS, SCARVES, HATS, BASEBALL BATS AND 26,000 CANS OF BEER.

EXCELLENT! DRESSED IN THESE OUTFITS OUR PLAYERS WILL BE ABLE TO MINGLE WITH THE GENUINE FULCHESTER SUPPORTERS.

BUT, WITH OUR MINDS POISONED BY ALCOHOL, WE WILL BEHAVE LIKE ANIMALS, BRINGING THUGGERY, VIOLENCE AND DESTRUCTION ONTO THE STREETS OF GDAZA!

BY THE END OF THE DAY THE AUTHORITIES WILL HAVE NO CHOICE BUT TO BAN FULCHESTER UNITED FROM ALL COMPETITIONS!

HA HA HA HA! GLUG GLUG GLUG!!

THE NEXT MORNING FULCHESTER BOARDED THEIR PLANE FOR BOTSLAVIA.

THE LADS HAVEN'T TRAINED FOR 2 DAYS. THEY'RE OUT OF CONDITION.

NOT TO WORRY. I TOOK THE PRECAUTION OF HAVING A DOZEN EXERSIZE BIKES LOADED ON BOARD. BY THE TIME WE REACH DISTANT BOTSLAVIA THE LADS WILL BE IN TIP-TOP CONDITION.

SOON FULCHESTER WERE AIRBORNE

AT THE END OF NINETY MINUTES IT'LL BE THE TEAM THAT SCORES THE MOST GOALS THAT'LL WIN THE GAME

IT'S A FUNNY GAME. ELEVEN MEN AGAINST ELEVEN MEN. IF WE GO OUT THERE AND PLAY FOOTBALL, WE'RE IN WITH A CHANCE AT THE END OF THE DAY. WHAT DO YOU THINK, SYD?

SYD? ARE YOU ALRIGHT?

WAIT A MOMENT!!

THIS ISN'T COACH SYD PRESTON! THIS IS A LIFE-SIZE DUMMY, PACKED WITH EXPLOSIVES!!

AND IT'S SET TO GO OFF AT ANY MOMENT!!

SOMEWHERE OVER THE NORTH SEA...

KABOOM!!

IS THIS THE END FOR FULCHESTER UNITED? AND WHAT WILL BECOME OF THE MARTIAN'S PLAN? IS THE UNACCEPTABLE FACE OF BRITISH SOCCER ABOUT TO REAR IT'S HEAD ON THE STREETS OF BOTSLAVIA? *DON'T MISS THE NEXT ISSUE!*

BILLY the FISH

EN ROUTE TO A VITAL EUROPEAN CUP TIE IN DISTANT BOTSLAVIA, FISH-BOY WONDER BILLY THOMSON AND HIS FULCHESTER TEAM-MATES BECAME THE UNSUSPECTING VICTIMS OF TERRORISM WHEN THEIR COACH, SYD PRESTON, EXPLODED.

OH NO! A BOMB!! THIS WILL REALLY PUT THE CAT AMONG THE PIDGEONS AS FAR AS TONIGHT'S TEAM SELECTION IS CONCERNED!

ARRRGH!!!

SECONDS LATER, IN THE RAGING SWELL OF THE NORTH SEA, FULCHESTER BOSS TOMMY BROWN HAS AN IDEA...

IT'S A GOOD JOB I ORDERED THESE CRATES, CONTAINING EXCERSIZE BIKES, TO BE LOADED ON BOARD. WE CAN USE THEM TO MAKE A BOAT. COME ON LADS, LET'S GET TO WORK.

SHORTLY...

WELL DONE LADS. A USEFUL BIT OF BOAT BUILDING.

BUT IT MAY STILL TAKE US SEVERAL HOURS TO REACH BOTSLAVIA, AND IF WE MISS THE KICK-OFF, OUR GOAL WILL BE LEFT AT THE MERCY OF THE BOTSLAVIAN FORWARDS!

SOMEONE IS GOING TO HAVE TO SWIM TO BOTSLAVIA AHEAD OF US AND HOLD THE FORT UNTIL WE ARRIVE.

I'LL GO!

YES BILLY. YOUR UNIQUE FISH-LIKE ABILITIES MAKE YOU THE OBVIOUS CHOICE. BUT BE CAREFUL!

BORN HALF-MAN, HALF-FISH, THOMSON WAS IDEALLY SUITED TO THE TASK IN HAND...

REMEMBER BILLY, KEEP IT TIGHT IN THE MIDDLE OF THE PARK, AND TRY TO CLOSE DOWN YOUR OPPONENT'S SPACE UNTIL THE REST OF THE TEAM ARRIVE.

OKAY BOSS.

MEANWHILE ON A FERRY SOMEWHERE IN THE NORTH SEA, EVIL GUS PARKER, BOSS OF RIVALS GRIMTHORPE CITY, HAS HIS OWN PLANS FOR FULCHESTER UNITED...

IN THE BAR...

RIGHT! THAT'S FIFTY-EIGHT PINTS I'VE HAD SO FAR!

ME TOO BOSS!

BY THE TIME WE REACH BOTSLAVIA WE'LL BE SO DRUNK AND BADLY BEHAVED THAT OUR ACTIONS WILL EARN FULCHESTER UNITED A **TOTAL BAN** FROM ALL EUROPEAN COMPETITIONS!

ALL PASSENGERS PLEASE COLLECT YOUR BAGGAGE AND PREPARE TO DISEMBARK.

SPLENDID! WE'RE HERE AT LAST. DRINK UP! NOW IT'S TIME TO **RUN AMOK** THROUGH THE QUIET STREETS OF BOTSLAVIA!!

SECONDS LATER...

HERE WE GO, HERE WE GO, HERE WE GO!

OUT OF MY WAY, GRANDAD!

UH?

S.S. BOTSLAV

WILL TOMMY BROWN'S TEAM REACH THE GDAZA STADIUM IN TIME FOR THE SECOND HALF? AND IS BILLY BOTSLAVIA BOUND? *DON'T MISS ISSUE 20!*

BILLY the FISH

DESPITE BEING BORN HALF-MAN, HALF-FISH, YOUNG BILLY THOMSON HAD MADE THE GOALKEEPER'S JERSEY AT FULCHESTER UNITED HIS OWN.

CD 7-86

STRANDED AT SEA EN ROUTE TO THEIR EUROPEAN CUP TIE IN DISTANT BOTSLAVIA, FULCHESTER BOSS TOMMY BROWN HAD SENT 'FISH BOY' WONDER BILLY THOMSON ON AHEAD TO KICK-OFF IN THEIR MATCH AGAINST BONGO GDAZA. OUTNUMBERED ELEVEN TO ONE, THOMSON'S BRILLIANT FIRST-HALF DISPLAY HAD EARNED HIS SIDE A HALF-TIME LEAD OF ONE GOAL TO NIL. BUT BONGO BOSS TELLY VEGETABLES IS SET TO MAKE A HALF-TIME TRANSFER SWOOP!

THOMSON. I WANT YOU TO SIGN FOR BONGO, FOR £10 MILLION!!

I'M QUITE HAPPY WHERE I AM... BUT I SUPPOSE I DO HAVE MY FAMILY TO CONSIDER...

I'LL GIVE YOU AN EXTRA MILLION IN CASH. PLUS FOUR HOUSES.

OKAY. IT'S A DEAL

WELCOME TO BONGO GDAZA! JUST SIGN HERE, AND WHEN THE SECOND HALF KICKS-OFF YOU'LL BE A BONGO PLAYER!

BUT... BILLY THOMSON. AS A PART-TIME MEMBER OF THE BOTSLAVIAN SECRET SERVICE, I ARREST YOU FOR SPYING.

WHAT THE...?

YOU HAVE JUST SIGNED A WRITTEN CONFESSION TO CRIMES PERPETRATED AGAINST THE BOTSLAVIAN STATE!

GUARDS. TAKE HIM AWAY.

YOU WON'T GET AWAY WITH THIS!

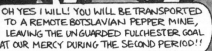

OH YES I WILL! YOU WILL BE TRANSPORTED TO A REMOTE BOTSLAVIAN PEPPER MINE, LEAVING THE UNGUARDED FULCHESTER GOAL AT OUR MERCY DURING THE SECOND PERIOD!!

SOON THE SECOND HALF IS UNDERWAY...

WITH NO OPPOSITION AT ALL, WE SHOULD BE ABLE TO DOMINATE THE GAME IN THE NEXT CRUCIAL 45 MINUTES.

THIS IS AN IDEAL OPPORTUNITY FOR US TO REVERSE OUR ONE GOAL DEFECIT!

BUT WITH BONGO NOW THE CLEAR FAVOURITES, THE PRESSURE ON THEM BEGINS TO TELL...

OH NO! I'VE MISSED AN OPEN GOAL!

BOO!

WHAT A LOAD OF RUBBISH!

OOPS!

AFTER A STRING OF MISSED CHANCES AND WITH ONLY SECONDS REMAINING, BONGO ARE STILL A GOAL BEHIND.

AGGH! I'M UNDER SO MUCH PRESSURE TO DO WELL I CAN HARDLY CONTROL THE BALL!

UH!

A FINAL CHANCE FALLS TO THE BONGO CAPTAIN

THIS COULD BE OUR LAST CHANCE. I MUST MAKE IT COUNT.

AT LAST, HERE COMES THE EQUALIZER!

TAP!

BUT AS HIS EFFORT APPROACHES THE FULCHESTER NET.

SAVED ON THE LINE!

BOOT!

DAMN! FULCHESTER HAVE ARRIVED AT THE ELEVENTH HOUR

GOSH! IT LOOKS LIKE WE GOT HERE JUST IN TIME, LADS

AND AS THE FINAL WHISTLE BLEW

WELL TOMMY. WE WON ONE - NIL

YES, A GOOD RESULT UNDER THE CIRCUMSTANCES. BUT WHAT HAS BECOME OF BILLY THOMSON, OUR VANISHING FISH-LIKE KEEPER?

MEANWHILE, IN A REMOTE PEPPER MINE IN BLEAK NORTHERN BOTSLAVIA...

BILLY THOMSON?

YES

A LETTER FOR YOU

PEPPER

I DON'T BELIEVE IT! IT'S FROM ENGLAND SUPREMO ROBBIE BOBSON. HE'S CHOSEN ME TO PLAY FOR ENGLAND... TOMORROW!

WILL BILLY ESCAPE IN TIME TO MAKE HIS INTERNATIONAL DEBUT, OR IS THIS THE END OF HIS FOOTBALL CAREER? – SEE ISSUE 21!

Oh dear. We've just realised that due to the unusual shape of the above strip we're left with a rather large and embarrassing gap in the bottom half of this page. So we've decided to have a **'Spot the Difference'** competition.

The above episode of Billy the Fish has been repeated below, but our artists have made a few slight changes. Can you spot what they are? Write down as many as you can, then turn to the very last page for the answers. Or alternatively skip this rather half hearted attempt at a competition and go straight on to the next page.

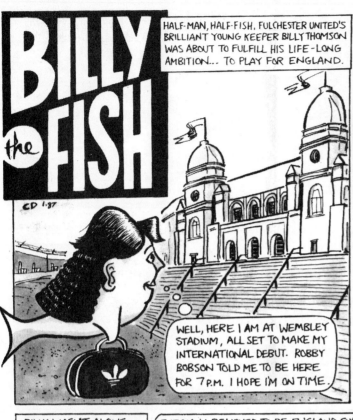

BILLY the FISH

CD 1·87

HALF-MAN, HALF-FISH, FULCHESTER UNITED'S BRILLIANT YOUNG KEEPER BILLY THOMSON WAS ABOUT TO FULFILL HIS LIFE-LONG AMBITION... TO PLAY FOR ENGLAND.

WELL, HERE I AM AT WEMBLEY STADIUM, ALL SET TO MAKE MY INTERNATIONAL DEBUT. ROBBY BOBSON TOLD ME TO BE HERE FOR 7 P.M. I HOPE I'M ON TIME.

IN THE CHANGING ROOMS...

STRANGE, THERE'S NOBODY HERE!

EVERYONE ELSE MUST HAVE ALREADY CHANGED. I'D BETTER GET A MOVE ON.

BUT AS BILLY EMERGED FROM THE FAMOUS PLAYERS TUNNEL ONTO THE FAMOUS WEMBLEY TURF

UH?

THE GROUND IS COMPLETELY EMPTY. IT LOOKS AS IF I HAVE BEEN THE VICTIM OF A CRUEL HOAX!

BILLY WASN'T ALONE...

HOSE PIPE WATER VALVE

THE MAN I BELIEVED TO BE ENGLAND SUPREMO ROBBY BOBSON MUST HAVE BEEN AN EVIL YET TALENTED IMPRESSIONIST. BUT WHY LURE ME HERE, TO WEMBLEY STADIUM?

EXIT

THAT'S ODD! THE DOORS ARE LOCKED.

OH NO! THE STADIUM HAS BEEN LOCKED AND THAT HOSE HAS BEEN LEFT RUNNING! SOON THE WATER LEVEL INSIDE THE GROUND WILL BEGIN TO RISE... AND RISE... AND I'LL BE DROWNED!!!

MEANWHILE, AFTER THE SHOCK DISMISSAL OF TEAM BOSS TOMMY BROWN, FULCHESTER CHAIRMAN RICK SPANGLE ACTS SWIFTLY TO APPOINT A SUCCESSOR.

FULCHESTER UNITED FOOTBALL CLUB HAS GOT GREAT POTENTIAL, I ENJOY A CHALLENGE, I PLAY GOLF, AND I'VE ALWAYS WANTED TO BE A FOOTBALL MANAGER.

WELL, MR... ERM... SMITH, YOU'VE GOT THE JOB!

SHORTLY...

MR SMITH, I'D LIKE YOU TO MEET OUR TEAM COACH SYD PRESTON. SYD HAS BEEN WITH THE CLUB FOR 26 YEARS.

HELLO MR SMITH

I'M SURE I'VE SEEN THAT FACE BEFORE

I'VE GOT BIG PLANS FOR THIS CLUB, PRESTON. BUT YOU DON'T FIGURE IN THEM. YOU'RE FIRED.

BUT...

YOU'RE TRESSPASSING ON FULCHESTER UNITED PROPERTY! GET OUT OR I'LL CALL THE POLICE.

MOMENTS LATER THE NEW BOSS IS AT HIS DESK...

BY THE TIME I'VE FINISHED MY STINT AS MANAGER, FULCHESTER UNITED WILL BE BOTTOM OF THE FIRST DIVISION, AND GRIMTHORPE CITY WILL BE UN-CHALLENGED AS THEY BID FOR THE FIRST DIVISION CHAMPIONSHIP!

HA! JUST AS I THOUGHT. THE MYSTERIOUS 'MR. SMITH' IS IN FACT NONE OTHER THAN...

...GUS PARKER, THE EVIL BOSS OF OUR ARCH RIVALS GRIMTHORPE CITY!!

IT WASN'T LONG TILL PARKER WAS IN ACTION... ON THE TRANSFER MARKET.

HELLO? IS THAT FOURTH DIVISION NO-HOPERS PEDDLEWORTH ALBION? THIS IS MR J. SMITH, THE NEW BOSS AT FULCHESTER UNITED.

I'D LIKE TO SWAP ALL OF OUR BEST PLAYERS FOR SOME OF YOUR WORST ONES.

AND I'LL THROW IN OUR BRILLIANT KEEPER BILLY THOMSON FREE OF CHARGE!

MEANWHILE AT WEMBLEY STADIUM THINGS ARE BEGINNING TO LOOK GRIM FOR BILLY...

HELP! HELP!!

IS WEMBLEY STADIUM SET TO BECOME A WATERY GRAVE FOR THE YOUNG FULCHESTER NUMBER ONE? AND IS HE REALLY SET TO JOIN NO-HOPERS PEDDLEWORTH TOWN ON A FREE TRANSFER? DON'T MISS ISSUE 23!

BILLY the FISH

TRAPPED INSIDE A FLOODING WEMBLEY STADIUM, FULCHESTER'S BRILLIANT 'FISH LIKE' GOALKEEPER BILLY THOMSON WAS UNAWARE THAT GUS PARKER, EVIL BOSS OF GRIMTHORPE CITY, HAD BEEN APPOINTED MANAGER AT FULCHESTER STADIUM AFTER THE SHOCK DISMISSAL OF TOMMY BROWN, AND THAT PARKER, DETERMINED TO WRECK FULCHESTER'S CHANCES OF SUCCESS, HAD BEEN SELLING OFF THE CLUB'S BEST PLAYERS.

IN A NEARBY AIR-SEA RESCUE HELICOPTER

HEY LOOK! AN S.O.S. SIGNAL. IT LOOKS LIKE SOMEONE'S IN TROUBLE AT WEMBLEY STADIUM!

WHY IT'S BILLY THOMSON, THE BRILLIANT FULCHESTER NO.1

BOY, AM I GLAD TO SEE YOU!

CD 287

OH NO! OH NO! THE WATER LEVEL IS RISING FAST. ANOTHER FEW INCHES AND IT COULD BE CURTAINS FOR ME... UNLESS I CAN JUST REACH THAT FLOODLIGHT.

BUT BILLY WASN'T SO GLAD TO HEAR THAT HE, ALONG WITH THE ENTIRE FULCHESTER TEAM, HAD BEEN SOLD TO FOURTH DIVISION NO-HOPERS PEDDLEWORTH ALBION...

THE NEXT DAY

WELL, HERE WE ARE AT LOWLY PEDDLEWORTH PARK. OUR NEW HOME!

YES. NOTHING COULD BE FURTHER FROM THE BRIGHT LIGHTS OF FULCHESTER STADIUM

WELCOME TO PEDDLEWORTH ALBION!

TOMMY BROWN - OUR FORMER FULCHESTER BOSS - SURELY YOU'RE NOT NOW IN CHARGE HERE AT PEDDLEWORTH ALBION?

YES. I GOT THE JOB THIS MORNING. WITH YOUR TALENT AND MY FOOTBALL BRAIN, WE'RE GOING TO PUT UNFASHIONABLE PEDDLEWORTH BACK ON THE FOOTBALL MAP!

MEET BROWN FOX, THE PEDDLEWORTH CAPTAIN. FROM NOW ON YOU'LL BE PLAYING ALONGSIDE HER.

ORPHANED IN A PLANE CRASH, SHE WAS RAISED IN THE JUNGLE BY A TRIBE OF FOOTBALLING INDIANS.

SHE'S GOT A USEFUL LEFT FOOT!

AND I'D LIKE YOU TO MEET... OOF!!....

BOP!

SORRY BOSS!

.... JOHNNY X, PEDDLEWORTH'S TOP SCORER. HE'S BEEN INVISIBLE SINCE A CHILDHOOD LABORATORY ACCIDENT IN WHICH HIS FATHER, A BRILLIANT SCIENTIST, WAS KILLED.

WACK!!

A REDSKIN WINGER AND AN INVISIBLE TARGET MAN! THEY COULD FORGE A USEFUL PARTNERSHIP UP FRONT.

BILLY'S PEDDLEWORTH DEBUT CAME LATER THAT WEEK AT HOME TO UNFASHIONABLE BAGSLEY THISTLE.

WITH BILLY THE FISH ON OUR SIDE PEDDLEWORTH WILL BE LOOKING TO TAKE 3 POINTS FROM THIS AFTERNOON'S VISITORS.

COME ALONG THE ALBION!

YES. NEW BOSS TOMMY BROWN WILL BE DISAPPOINTED WITH ANYTHING LESS FROM THIS, HIS FIRST GAME IN CHARGE.

BUT ALL THE ACTION WAS IN THE OPPONENT'S GOALMOUTH

WHAT A RUN BY THE LARGE BREASTED REDSKIN WINGER!

AND WHAT A CROSS TOO!

PITTY THERE'S NO-ONE AT THE FAR POST TO CONVERT IT!

OH YES THERE IS!

UH?

GOAL!!

BONK!

A CLINICAL FINISH FROM THE INVISIBLE STRIKER!

THE NEXT DAY TOMMY BROWN IS CELEBRATING PEDDLEWORTH'S TEN-NIL VICTORY WHEN...

THAT WIN LIFTS US OFF THE BOTTOM OF THE TABLE TOMMY.

YES! BUT HAVE YOU SEEN THE FRONT PAGE?!

SUNDAY SHITE

BILLY THOMSON IS ON HEROIN!

IS BILLY ON HEROIN? DON'T MISS ISSUE 24!

BILLY THE FISH!

DESPITE BEING BORN HALF MAN, HALF FISH, YOUNG GOALKEEPER BILLY THOMSON WAS DETERMINED TO MAKE IT TO THE TOP...

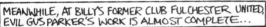

THE ARRIVAL OF BILLY THOMSON AND HIS FORMER FULCHESTER TEAM MATES WAS WORKING WONDERS FOR FOURTH DIVISION STRUGGLERS PEDDLEWORTH ALBION WHO HAD JUST WON THEIR FIRST GAME IN 8 YEARS. BUT THE NEXT DAY, BILLY IS CALLED IN TO SEE BOSS TOMMY BROWN

IF THIS IS TRUE BILLY YOU'VE PLAYED YOUR LAST GAME FOR PEDDLEWORTH ALBION!

SUNDAY SHITE
BILLY THOMSON IS ON HEROIN

BUT BOSS, THIS IS A **DIFFERENT** BILLY THOMSON. THE ARTICLE REFERS TO BILLY THOMSON THE OUTRAGEOUS POP SINGER, ALSO KNOWN AS 'BOY WILLIAM'!

HEROIN
BOY WILLIAM IN DRUGS SWOOP

SO IT DOES. SORRY BILLY. MY MISTAKE.

MEANWHILE, AT BILLY'S FORMER CLUB FULCHESTER UNITED, EVIL GUS PARKER'S WORK IS ALMOST COMPLETE...

HERE, I'LL GIVE YOU TEN MILLION QUID FOR THIS LORRY LOAD OF PENSIONERS.

GOLDEN PASTURES OLD FOGIES HOMES

TEN MILLION! IT'S A DEAL!!!

HA HA HA! AFTER ONLY A WEEK IN CHARGE OF FULCHESTER THEY'RE BOTTOM OF DIVISION ONE! I'VE SOLD OFF ALL THEIR PLAYERS, AND REPLACED THEM WITH PENSIONERS. NOT SURPRISINGLY, ATTENDANCES ARE DOWN FROM 40,000 INTO SINGLE FIGURES!

HEH HEH HEH!

WITHIN A MONTH FULCHESTER WILL GO BUST!

AND WITH THEM OUT OF THE WAY FOR GOOD, I WILL RETURN TO GRIMTHORPE CITY AND WIN THE LEAGUE!

AH-HA! AH-HA! AH-HA!

THE NEXT DAY PEDDLEWORTH ARE PREPARING FOR THEIR MIDWEEK VISIT TO HIGH FLYING REDHURST ROVERS...

AH! HERE IT IS BOSS. REDHURST. IT'S ABOUT 240 MILES AWAY.

GOOD WORK SID. WE SIMPLY **MUST** GET A RESULT AT REDHURST TOMORROW NIGHT IN ORDER TO EASE OUR RELEGATION WORRIES.

A WEEK IS A LONG TIME IN FOOTBALL. THREE POINTS TOMORROW, FOLLOWED BY A RESULT ON SATURDAY, WOULD PUT US IN WITH A GOOD CHANCE OF PROMOTION!

WEDNESDAY ARRIVED...

IS EVERYONE ON THE COACH, SID?

YES, THAT'S THE LOT.

BUT...

OH NO! THE MAP! I'VE LOST IT!!

NO MAP, AND ONLY THREE HOURS TO GET TO REDHURST. WE'LL NEVER FIND THE PLACE!

THINGS LOOKED GRIM UNTIL REDSKIN WINGER BROWN FOX STEPPED IN...

ME FIND REDHURST! YOU FOLLOW.

OF COURSE! WITH HER NATURAL HUNTING AND TRACKING INSTINCTS BROWN FOX WILL BE ABLE TO LEAD US TO REDHURST.

AN HOUR OR SO LATER...

IT CAN'T BE MUCH FURTHER NOW

REDHURST 30

SURE ENOUGH, THE REMARKABLE REDSKIN WINGER LEAD HER TEAM-MATES TO REDHURST ROAD...

IT LOOKS LIKE WE'RE JUST IN TIME

REDHURST

AS THE GAME GOT UNDERWAY IT NEEDED ALL OF BILLY'S FISH-LIKE BRILLIANCE TO KEEP THE HIGH FLYING REDHURST FORWARDS AT BAY

THIS SCORCHING EFFORT LOOKS UNSTOPABLE!

INCREDIBLE!

YES! IT MUST BE 1-0 TO ROVERS!

ABSOLUTELY! IT LOOKS A GOAL ALL THE WAY!

THE BOY THOMSON WAS EQUAL TO IT!! WHAT A SAVE!

BUT, WITH LESS THAN A MINUTE TO GO, REDHURST'S Nº9 FINDS HIMSELF WITH ONLY THE KEEPER TO BEAT.

HE'S ROUNDED THE FISH GOALIE!

CRUMBS! I'VE BEEN BEATEN ON THE EDGE OF MY 18 YARD AREA. IF HE SCORES, IT'S ALL OVER!

THERE WERE SOME ANXIOUS FACES ON THE PEDDLEWORTH BENCH...

OH NO! BILLY'S LEFT HIM WITH AN OPEN GOAL!

I DOUBT IF EVEN THE LIGHTENING PACE OF OUR BUXOM REDSKIN WINGER CAN SAVE US NOW. SHE'S A FULL 90 YARDS AWAY FROM THE BALL!

CAN BROWN FOX GET BACK IN TIME TO ROB REDHURST OF VICTORY? OR IS IT ALL OVER FOR BILLY'S TEAM? DON'T MISS ISSUE 25

Billy the Fish

DESPITE BEING BORN HALF-MAN, HALF-FISH, ETC. ETC...

PLAYING FOR FOURTH DIVISION STRUGGLERS PEDDLEWORTH ALBION, BOY-FISH WONDER BILLY THOMSON HAD BEEN BEATEN ON THE EDGE OF HIS 18 YARD AREA IN THE FINAL MINUTE OF A VITAL CUP CLASH WITH HIGH FLYING REDHURST ROVERS. A GOAL LOOKED CERTAIN....

HAH! I GOBBLE UP CHANCES LIKE THESE!

OH NO! A GOAL AT THIS STAGE OF THE GAME WOULD MAKE THE SCORE ONE-NIL

YES BOSS, AND IT WOULD LEAVE US WITH A MOUNTAIN TO CLIMB.

IT'S THERE!

A TAP IN!

A GOAL, SURELY!

BUT...

WHIZZZZZ! BANG!

UH?

A BRILLIANT SAVE, BROWN FOX. THAT WELL AIMED ARROW HAS SAVED THE DAY FOR PEDDLEWORTH!

FOILED BY A DEAD-EYE REDSKIN!

WITH ONLY SECONDS TO GO, BILLY PUMPS A LONG BALL UP THE MIDDLE OF THE PARK.

THUD!

I'LL WIN THIS DUEL IN THE AIR BY HOLDING MY OPPONENT DOWN

MAN ON!

BUT...

UH?

WELL PLAYED JOHNNY X!

A DEFT TOUCH BY THE INVISIBLE TARGET MAN STRAIGHT TO THE FEET OF THE LONG-LEGGED REDSKIN WINGER!

COME ON THE ALBION!

THE FULL NINETY MINUTES ARE UP ON MY WATCH

YES BOSS. WE'RE NOW ENTERING TIME ADDED ON FOR STOPPAGES

LIKE A STREAK OF SILVER LIGHTENING THE LARGE BREASTED REDSKIN BEAUTY DARTED FORWARD TOWARDS THE DEAD BALL LINE....

THIS BAREFOOT REDSKIN IS RUNNING RINGS AROUND US!

MAGNIFICENT SKILLS FROM THE WELL ENDOWED WINGER

BUT WILL SHE MAKE HER FINAL BALL A TELLING ONE?

OH DEAR. SHE SEEMS TO HAVE HIT IT TOO DEEP!

BUT...

BLAM!

OOOOF!!

IT'S A GOAL!

WHAT A THUNDERBOLT!

BUT NO! THE INVISIBLE NUMBER NINE HAS RUN ALL OF FIFTY YARDS TO MEET THE CROSS WITH A THUNDEROUS VOLLEY!

PEDDLEWORTH CELEBRATE THEIR LAST MINUTE VICTORY WITH A HOT BATH...

GOOD WORK BROWN FOX.

YES, A TERRIFIC RUN AND CROSS

BUT THEY ARE NOT ALONE IN THE BATH...

WHAT EVIL LURKS BENEATH THE MURKY WATERS OF THE PEDDLEWORTH PLAYERS' HOT BATH? **ALL IS REVEALED** IN ISSUE 26!!!

BILLY the FISH

MAN-FISH MIRACLE BILLY THOMSON AND HIS PEDDLEWORTH ALBION TEAM MATES ARE CELEBRATING A REMARKABLE LAST MINUTE VICTORY AGAINST REDHURST ROVERS WITH A WELL EARNED HOT BATH, WHEN SUDDENLY...

DESPITE BEING BORN HALF MAN, HALF FISH, ETC. ETC. ETC.

LOOK OUT BILLY! / SHARK ATTACK!! / CRIKEY!

DON'T PANIC! THIS IS A NURSE SHARK. A SMALL AND RELATIVELY HARMLESS FISH OFTEN FOUND IN SHALLOW WATER / PHEW!

THE NEXT DAY... / WELL SID, YESTERDAY'S WIN PUTS US IN WITH A GOOD CHANCE OF PROMOTION. / YES BOSS, THE LADS DONE MAGNIFICENT / WE ONLY NEED TO TAKE FIVE POINTS FROM OUR ONE REMAINING FIXTURE TO BE SURE OF PROMOTION!

FIVE POINTS... I THOUGHT THE MOST YOU COULD GET WAS THREE? / DAMN IT SID, YOU'RE RIGHT! THAT LEAVES US WITH A MOUNTAIN TO CLIMB!

BUT LOOK AT THIS... OUR FORMER CLUB, FULCHESTER UNITED, ARE IN DEEP FINANCIAL TROUBLE! / SFORT / FULCHESTER UNITED IN DEEP FINANCIAL TROUBLE! / MANAGER QUITS

PERHAPS I COULD GIVE THEM A RING AND ARRANGE A MERGER BETWEEN OUR TWO CLUBS...

THE NEXT MORNING TOMMY BROWN IS BACK IN HIS OLD OFFICE- AS THE MANAGER OF NEWLY FORMED 'FULCHESTER ALBION'...

THERE WE ARE. PEDDLEWORTH'S POINTS, WHEN ADDED TO FIRST DIVISION FULCHESTER'S, LEAVE OUR NEW CLUB 'FULCHESTER ALBION' SECOND TOP OF THE LEAGUE / AND IF WE WIN OUR ONE REMAINING GAME- AT HOME TO TOP CLUB GRIMTHORPE CITY (OUR ARCH RIVALS)... / NICE WORK BOSS! / ...WE'LL BE THE LEAGUE CHAMPIONS!

FOOTBALL LEAGUE DIV. ONE
1. GRIMTHORPE CITY 83
2. FULCHESTER ALBION 82
3. ROSSDALE ROVERS 76
PLUMFIELD THURSDAY
INKLEY ARGY

DAILY BILGE! / BIG HEADLINE ABOUT FOX

BUT TOMMY'S OPPOSITE NUMBER, EVIL GUS PARKER IS CONFIDENT OF A GRIMTHORPE VICTORY... / ON SATURDAY GRIMTHORPE WILL WIN THE LEAGUE... / SLAM! / AND NO FISH, LARGE BREASTED INDIAN OR INVISIBLE STRIKER IS GOING TO STOP US!!

ON THE EVE OF THE BIG MATCH TOMMY BROWN IS PUTTING THE FINISHING TOUCHES TO FULCHESTER'S PREPARATIONS. / LET'S KEEP IT TIGHT AT THE BACK AND PUSH IT ABOUT A BIT IN THE MIDDLE OF THE PARK / MY BALL!!!

F-NERK!

BAD NEWS! I THINK HE'S PULLED A VENTRAL FIN! HE COULD BE OUT OF ACTION FOR SIX WEEKS! / BROWN FOX SORRY. UM FIFTY-FIFTY BALL. / UGH! GROAN! / OH NO! WITHOUT BILLY WE'LL HAVE A MOUNTAIN TO CLIMB ON SATURDAY!

ON THE DAY OF THE BIG MATCH FULCHESTER STADIUM IS BUZZING WITH EXCITEMENT... / HAVE YOU HEARD THE NEWS? BILLY THOMSON IS OUT! / OH NO! THERE GO ALBION'S CHANCES!

AND IN THE GRIMTHORPE CHANGING ROOM / HA! WITH FISH FEATURES OUT OF ACTION WE'RE HOME AND DRY. BY QUARTER TO FIVE THIS AFTERNOON THE CHAMPIONSHIP WILL BE OURS! / HEH HEH HEH!

BUT AS THE TEAMS EMERGE... / IT CAN'T BE! / IT IS! / UNBELIEVABLE! / I DON'T BELIEVE IT!!

BILLY THOMSON IS PLAYING... ...ON CRUTCHES!!! / YES, AND WE LOOK SET FOR A THRILLING CLIMAX TO THE SEASON!

CAN BILLY OVERCOME HIS INJURY TO HELP FULCHESTER LIFT THE CHAMPIONSHIP? DON'T MISS THE ALL-ACTION CLIMAX IN THE NEXT ISSUE!?!

BILLY the FISH

BORN HALF MAN, HALF FISH, AN INCREDIBLE GOD GIVEN GOALKEEPING TALENT HAD NEVER-THE-LESS ENABLED YOUNG BILLY THOMSON TO MAKE THE N°1 JERSEY AT FULCHESTER HIS VERY OWN...

BOY/FISH FOOTBALL GENIUS BILLY THOMSON AND HIS FULCHESTER TEAM MATES NEED TO WIN THEIR FINAL GAME OF THE SEASON AT HOME TO ARCH RIVALS GRIMTHORPE CITY IN ORDER TO WIN THE LEAGUE. DESPITE A BADLY STRAINED FIN, BILLY HAS ELECTED TO PLAY... **ON CRUTCHES!**

AS THE TEAMS WARM UP BILLY IS IN OBVIOUS PAIN.

ARE YOU SURE YOU'RE OKAY BILLY?

D-D-DON'T WORRY ABOUT M-ME... I'LL... I'LL... BE FINE

BACK ON THE BENCH...

THE LAD THOMSON'S GOT A BIG HEART BOSS!

HE'S GOT COURAGE. HE'LL GO OUT THERE AND GIVE 110% FOR THE FULL NINETY MINUTES!

BUT AS THE GAME GETS UNDERWAY, THOMSON IS QUICKLY SINGLED OUT FOR ATTENTION BY THE BUSTLING GRIMTHORPE FORWARDS...

SLAM!!

THUD!

FREE KICK!?

OOF!

COME ON REF!

ERGH!

THOMSON IS TAKING A LOT OF PUNISHMENT FROM THE GRIMTHORPE FORWARDS, BOSS.

YES, AND HE'S GETTING VERY LITTLE PROTECTION FROM THE REFEREE

SURELY THAT'S A FOUL?

BOOO!

PLAY ON LADS!

SMACK!

MEANWHILE THERE'S ACTION AT THE OTHER END...

NEAT FOOTWORK FROM BROWN FOX! SHE'S TOTALLY WRONG FOOTED THE CITY DEFENCE!

CHIP!

FLICK!

UH?

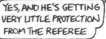

BRILLIANT ONE-TOUCH CONTROL BY JOHNNY X THE INVISIBLE STRIKER

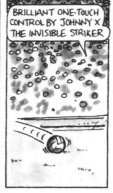

AMAZING SKILL! HE'S TURNING ON A SIXPENCE!

AND HE'S UNLEASHED A FERROCIOUS DRIVE!!

BOOT!

OOOOOH!!!

GRIMTHORPE ARE SAVED BY THE WOODWORK!

BUT CITY ARE QUICK TO REPLY...

I WONDER IF I SHOULD TRY MY LUCK FROM ALL OF 25 YARDS...

YOU KNOW WHAT THEY SAY, IF YOU DON'T BUY A TICKET, YOU WON'T WIN THE RAFFLE
← MANAGER'S VOICE

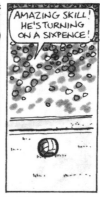

AND IT NEEDS A FINE SAVE FROM BILLY THOMSON TO KEEP THE SCORES LEVEL!

A FINE EFFORT

AND A FINE SAVE FROM THIS 'CAT LIKE' MAN/FISH MIRACLE!

LESS THAN A MINUTE TO GO UNTIL HALF-TIME AND THEY'RE STILL LEVEL. WHAT WOULDN'T FULCHESTER GIVE FOR A GOAL AT THIS VITAL STAGE!!

UP THE ALBION!

COME ON FULCHESTER!

MY! THIS IS REAL END-TO-END STUFF

YES. WHAT A MARVELLOUS ADVERT FOR OUR GAME!

THE REFEREE'S A BASTARD

SUDDENLY GRIMTHORPE BREAK AWAY ON THE LEFT FLANK...

OH NO! HE'S HEADING FOR THE DEAD-BALL LINE!

BUT...

DAMN! IT LOOKS AS IF I'VE WASTED MY CROSS!

THIS SHOULD POSE FULCHESTER NO PROBLEMS. THERE ISN'T A GRIMTHORPE PLAYER IN SIGHT.

THOMSON IS UNDER NO PRESSURE WHATSOEVER. HE SHOULD COLLECT THIS BALL EASILY.

YOUR BALL BILLY

A STRAIGHT-FORWARD ENOUGH CATCH FOR THE KEEPER!

OH! I DON'T BELIEVE IT!!

IT'S A DISASTER!!

AN OWN GOAL! THOMSON HAS SCORED FOR GRIMTHORPE ON THE STROKE OF HALF-TIME!

ARE GRIMTHORPE SET TO STEAL THE CHAMPIONSHIP FROM LUCKLESS FULCHESTER? OR CAN THE ALBION RECOVER FROM THIS SICKENING BLOW IN TIME TO SNATCH AN HISTORIC VICTORY? AND WHAT WILL TOMMY BROWN HAVE TO SAY TO HIS PLAYERS IN THE DRESSING ROOM AT HALF-TIME? *DON'T MISS THE NEXT ISSUE!*

Billy the Fish

DESPITE BEING BORN HALF-MAN, HALF-FISH, YOUNG GOALKEEPER BILLY THOMSON, ETC. ETC.

FULCHESTER UNITED NEED TO **WIN** THEIR FINAL GAME OF THE SEASON AT HOME TO ARCH RIVALS GRIMTHORPE CITY IN ORDER TO WIN THE LEAGUE. BUT A DISASTEROUS OWN GOAL BY INJURED KEEPER BILLY THOMSON HAS GIVEN THE VISITORS A HALF-TIME LEAD...

IN THE CHANGING ROOM...

WELL BILLY, THIS LEAVES US WITH A MOUNTAIN TO CLIMB

WHAT CAN I SAY BOSS? I'M AS SICK AS A PARROT!

HOW'S THE FIN BILLY? WILL YOU BE ABLE TO PLAY IN THE SECOND HALF?

IT LOOKS GRIM, SID

I CAN HARDLY MOVE IT!

WAIT UM MOMENT! BROWN FOX KNOW UM INDIAN HEALING DANCE. ME GNE IT A TRY BOSS?

GO ON THEN, BROWN FOX. IT'S OUR ONLY CHANCE!

AGADAGADUM DUM DUM DUM DUM!

AGA DOO DOO!

DUM DOO DOO! AGA DAGA DOO!

SHE'S CALLING ON THE GREAT HEALING SPIRITS TO RISE UP FROM THE EARTH AND CURE THE LAD

SHORTLY...

WELL BILLY, HOW DOES IT FEEL?

GREAT, BOSS. GOOD AS NEW!

FLIP!

FLIP!

RIGHT! LET'S GET OUT THERE AND SHOW GRIMTHORPE WHAT WE'RE MADE OF!!

FULCHESTER GET OFF TO A FLYING START...

A PIN-POINT PASS!

THE DASHING LARGE BREASTED REDSKIN IS CLEAR ON THE LEFT!

BROWN FOX IS GOALWARD BOUND!

BUT...

COME ON REF! THAT'S A FOUL!

SHOVE!!

FREE KICK!!

UNITED ARE AWARDED A FREE KICK 2 YARDS OUT...

AN OPPORTUNITY, THEN, FOR UNITED. BUT IT WILL TAKE A TREMENDOUS EEFFORT TO BEAT THE KEEPER FROM THAT DISTANCE

GRIMTHORPE'S 5 MAN WALL SEEM TO HAVE THE ANGLES COVERED

BROWN FOX IS GOING TO TAKE IT

THE BUSTY REDSKIN IS SURE TO TRY A BANANA SHOT!

UNUSUAL! SHE'S BLASTED THE BALL **DOWNWARDS**, INTO THE GROUND!

HA! SHEER BRILLIANCE! HER POWERFUL DRIVE HAS **TUNNELLED** IT'S WAY BENEATH THE WALL!

A TOUCH OF CLASS!!

GOAL!!

WHAT A SPECTACULAR EFFORT!

BUT WITH THE SCORES LEVEL GRIMTHORPE STILL HAVE THE ADVANTAGE - NEEDING ONLY A DRAW TO REMAIN AHEAD OF FULCHESTER AND TO WIN THE LEAGUE TROPHY...

THEIR EVIL BOSS GUS PARKER ORDERED HIS SIDE TO TAKE NO CHANCES...

TAKE NO CHANCES

AND IN THE UNITED DUG-OUT MANAGER TOMMY BROWN LOOKS ANXIOUS

TIME IS RUNNING OUT SID

WHAT WOULDN'T I GIVE FOR A GOAL AT THIS STAGE!

WITH ONLY SECONDS LEFT, BILLY STARTS A MOVE FROM INSIDE HIS OWN 18 YARD BOX...

HERE BROWN FOX, BUT HURRY. THERE'S ONLY SECONDS LEFT!

THIS COULD BE UNITED'S LAST CHANCE!

BREAST BALL!!

SHE CONTROLLED THE BALL WITH HER BOSOMS. BREAST BALL. **PENALTY** TO GRIMTHORPE!

HOWAY REF?!!

PENALTY!

IS IT ALL OVER FOR FULCHESTER? WILL GRIMTHORPE SNATCH THE WINNER FROM THE PENALTY SPOT AND WIN THE TITLE? OR CAN UNITED POSSIBLY BE SAVED? IN THE NEXT ISSUE BILLY FACES HIS BIGGEST TEST!

BILLY the FISH

BORN HALF-MAN, HALF-FISH, YOUNG GOALKEEPER BILLY THOMSON BLAH BLAH BLAH ETC. ETC. NOW READ ON...

CD 2.88

IN THEIR FINAL GAME OF THE SEASON FULCHESTER UNITED MUST **BEAT** ARCH RIVALS GRIMTHORPE CITY IN ORDER TO WIN THE LEAGUE. BUT WITH THE SCORE AT 1-1, GRIMTHORPE HAVE BEEN AWARDED A CONTROVERSIAL PENALTY KICK IN THE FINAL MINUTE OF THE GAME. IT LOOKS LIKE THE END OF UNITED'S CHAMPIONSHIP DREAM

A DEATHLY HUSH DESCENDS ON FULCHESTER STADIUM...

COME ON BILLY! YOU CAN DO IT

I'LL HAVE TO PULL OFF THE GREATEST SAVE OF MY CAREER TO STOP THIS ONE

ON THE UNITED BENCH

IT'S ALL UP TO BILLY NOW. HE'S THE ONLY ONE WHO CAN SAVE US

YES, BUT A SAVE WON'T BE GOOD ENOUGH! WE ALSO NEED A GOAL AT THE OTHER END IN ORDER TO WIN IT, SID.

AND ON MY WATCH THERE'S LESS THAN 5 SECONDS TO GO!

IT'S GOING TO TAKE A MIRACLE TO SAVE US - OR A PIECE OF SHEER FISH-LIKE BRILLIANCE FROM BILLY THOMSON!

OH WELL... HERE GOES!

PHEEP!

I'M GOING TO HAVE TO MAKE A SPLIT SECOND DECISION...

DO I DIVE TO THE LEFT, OR TO THE RIGHT?

THUD!

WELL SID, THERE'S NOTHING WE CAN DO NOW BUT WAIT. THE BALL HAS BEEN KICKED. WILL BILLY BE ABLE TO REACH IT BEFORE IT CROSSES THE LINE?

I CAN'T BEAR TO WATCH!

BUT AS THE BALL HURTLES TOWARDS THE NET BILLY HAS ALREADY DIVED TO HIS **RIGHT**...

OH NO! IT'S GOING THE **OTHER WAY**!!

I'VE GOT TO SOMEHOW CHANGE DIRECTION BEFORE IT'S TOO LATE!

FLIP!

FLIP!

AGGH!!

FLIP! FLIP! FLIP!

WHAT A SAVE!

INCREDIBLE!

AMAZING STOP! HE **JUST** GOT HIS FIN TO IT IN THE NICK OF TIME!

A BREATHTAKING DISPLAY OF MID-AIR 'AQUABATICS' BY THE MAN/FISH MAESTRO!

THE RE-BOUND FALLS TO BROWN FOX ON THE EDGE OF THE 18 YARD AREA.

ME SEE JOHNNY X UNMARKED ON UM HALF-WAY LINE

ME FIND HIM WITH UM FIRST-TIME BALL

SPECTACULAR!

WHAT A BALL!

HER PIN-POINT PASS TURNS DEFENCE INTO ATTACK AS INVISIBLE STRIKER JOHNNY X RACES TOWARDS THE GRIMTHORPE GOAL...

THE LARGE BREASTED REDSKIN'S SUPERB BALL LEAVES JOHNNY X WITH ONLY THE GRIMTHORPE KEEPER TO BEAT!

SUPERB BALL CONTROL!

BUT JUST AS JOHNNY'S SHOT IS ABOUT TO CROSS THE LINE...

HE'S BEATEN THE KEEPER! SURELY THIS IS THE WINNER FOR UNITED

PHEEP!

OH NO! THE FULL-TIME WHISTLE. IT'S ALL OVER!

DID THE WHISTLE BLOW **BEFORE** THE BALL CROSSED THE LINE, OR WILL THE GOAL STAND, MAKING FULCHESTER UNITED CHAMPIONS OF THE FOOTBALL LEAGUE?

DON'T MISS THE NEXT ISSUE!

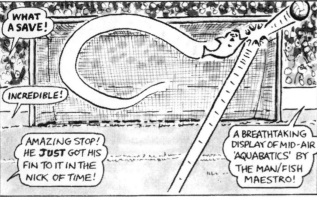

The balding academic Professor Wolfgang Schnell B.Sc., Ph.D., despatches a header goalward bound with trigonometrical precision correct to seven decimal places.

Guided by his trusty blind dog Shep, 84 year old veteran Rex Findlay rounds the keeper with ease.

Billy the Fish

FULCHESTER MUST WIN THEIR FINAL GAME OF THE SEASON AGAINST GRIMTHORPE TOWN IN ORDER TO WIN THE LEAGUE. IN THE DYING SECONDS, WITH THE SCORES LEVEL, FULCHESTER'S INVISIBLE STRIKER JOHNNY X SCORES WHAT LOOKS TO BE THE WINNER. BUT JUST AS THE BALL CROSSES THE LINE, THE FINAL WHISTLE BLOWS.....

DESPITE, ETC.

C.D.S.T.588

ALL EYES ARE ON THE REFEREE...

DID THE BALL CROSS THE LINE BEFORE OR AFTER THE WHISTLE BLEW?

THAT'S THE QUESTION

WELL REF? UM GOAL OR NOT?

OH SORRY LADS- I WAS JUST PRACTISING WITH MY WHISTLE. THERE'S STILL A MINUTE TO PLAY. THE GOAL STANDS.

GOAL!

HOORAY!

ONE MINUTE LATER...

THAT *IS* THE FINAL WHISTLE!

PEEP!

YES. VICTORY TO FULCHESTER

THE CELEBRATIONS BEGIN...

HOORAY FOR UNITED!

WELL DONE BILLY!

WE WON UM LEAGUE, WE WON UM LEAGUE, EE-AYE-ADIO, WE WON UM LEAGUE

JUBILANT SUPPORTERS STREAM ONTO THE PITCH...

HOORAY!

AMAZING SCENES HERE AT FULCHESTER STADIUM

WELL BOSS- WE'VE WON THE LEAGUE

YES SYD, IT LITERALLY HASN'T SUNK IN YET.

THAT NIGHT - UNITED CHAIRMAN RICK SPANGLE INVITES THE TEAM TO HIS FULCHESTER NIGHTCLUB FOR A CELEBRATION...

SPANGLES

INSIDE...

ENJOY YOURSELVES LADS, BUT I WANT YOU ALL IN BED BY NINE O'CLOCK.

DON'T FORGET - WE'VE GOT THE CUP FINAL TO WIN TOMORROW AFTERNOON.

SHORTLY...

HI. I'M TOP MODEL CINDY SMALLPIECE. CAN I BUY YOU A DRINK?

ACTUALLY, I'M A PROFESSIONAL SPORTSMAN SO I DON'T DRINK ALCOHOL, BUT I'D LOVE A WEAK CHERRYADE.

BUT, AT THE BAR...

ONE WEAK CHERRYADE PLEASE, SPIKED WITH HALF A BOTTLE OF WHISKY.

CERTAINLY MADAM

WELL BOSS, THE YOUNG LAD THOMSON IS CERTAINLY ENJOYING HIMSELF. JUST LOOK AT HIM GO!

YES, THE LAD'S QUITE A MOVER. I JUST HOPE HE DOESN'T INJURE HIMSELF- WE COULDN'T AFFORD TO BE WITHOUT HIM IN TOMORROW'S CUP FINAL.

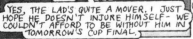

MEANWHILE, NOT FAR AWAY...

EXCUSE ME, BROWN FOX ISN'T IT?

MY NAME'S BOB BARNES- BOSS OF BARNTON WANDERERS, YOUR OPPONENTS IN THE CUP FINAL TOMORROW. I HAVE A FEW BEADS AND TRINKETS WHICH YOU MAY LIKE TO HAVE - IN RETURN FOR A SMALL FAVOUR...

HEY... I FEEL REALLY STRANGE! BUT I REALLY THINK I OUGHT TO BE GOING SOON, MISS SMALLPIECE - IT'S AFTER MY BEDTIME.

DON'T WORRY BILLY. I'LL GIVE YOU A LIFT. I HAVE MY EXPENSIVE RED SPORTSCAR OUTSIDE.

PRESENTLY...

I'LL TELL YOU WHAT BILLY. WHY NOT COME BACK TO MY PLACE.... FOR A CUP OF COFFEE.

THE NEXT DAY AT WEMBLEY, FULCHESTER ARE ABOUT TO KICK OFF IN THE CUP FINAL...

COME ON UNITED

BUT ONE PLAYER IS MISSING...

ONLY SECONDS TO GO, AND STILL NO SIGN OF BILLY THOMSON

HE'S CERTAINLY CUTTING IT FINE

WHERE ON EARTH CAN THOMSON BE, BOSS? IT'S NOT LIKE HIM TO BE LATE

THIS IS MOST UNUSUAL. BILLY IS NORMALLY THE IDEAL PROFESSIONAL

BUT- IN A FLAT MANY MILES AWAY...

COME ON BABY, LET'S DO IT AGAIN. ONE MORE TIME FOR BILLY?

BUT WHAT ABOUT THE CUP FINAL? SHOULDN'T YOU BE PLAYING?

THE CUP FINAL? FORGET IT. I'VE GOT BETTER THINGS TO DO TODAY THAN PLAY FOOTBALL!

BILLY the FISH

AT WEMBLEY STADIUM, LEAGUE CHAMPIONS FULCHESTER UNITED ARE SET TO KICK OFF IN THE F.A. CUP FINAL AGAINST BARNTON WANDERERS BUT **BILLY THOMSON**, THEIR INCREDIBLE HALF MAN, HALF FISH GOALKEEPER, IS SEVERAL MILES AWAY - IN BED WITH TOP MODEL **CINDY SMALLPIECE**.

I'M SICK OF PLAYING FOOTBALL. FROM NOW ON I ONLY WANT TO **PLAY WITH YOU** CINDY!

I'M AFRAID THAT WON'T BE POSSIBLE BILLY...

GUS PARKER! BOSS OF OUR ARCH RIVALS GRIMTHORPE CITY!

YES - AND I SUPPOSE YOU'RE WONDERING WHY I LURED YOU HERE IN THIS CLEVER CINDY SMALLPIECE DISGUISE...

QUITE SIMPLE! BLACKMAIL! I TOOK THESE PHOTOGRAPHS LAST NIGHT - SHOWING YOU IN A VARIETY OF COMPROMISING POSITIONS...

PERHAPS YOU'D LIKE TO BUY THEM... FOR £50,000!

NOT SO FAST PARKER! YOUR BLACKMAIL PLAN WON'T WORK... FOR ONE SIMPLE REASON!

OH YES? AND WHAT'S THAT?

HA! I'M **NOT** BILLY THE FISH, I'M TOMMY BROWN, THE UNITED BOSS!

I THOUGHT YOU'D TRY SOMETHING LIKE THIS, SO I WORE THIS CLEVER BILLY THOMSON DISGUISE TO PROTECT OUR FISH-LIKE KEEPER!

BUT **I'M** THE REAL BILLY THOMSON! I THOUGHT **YOU** WERE GUS PARKER DISGUISED AS ME ALL ALONG!

BILLY! IT WAS **YOU** I'M SORRY. THIS HAS ALL BEEN A BIG MISTAKE!

BUT IF **YOU'RE** BILLY THOMSON, AND I'M TOMMY BROWN, **WHO** IS SITTING ON THE BENCH AT WEMBLEY STADIUM DISGUISED AS ME?

I DON'T KNOW, BUT WE'D BETTER FIND OUT. THE CUP FINAL KICKS OFF ANY MINUTE NOW!

MINUTES LATER AT WEMBLEY STADIUM...

LOOK BOSS. HERE COMES BILLY, JUST IN TIME, AND LOOK WHO'S WITH HIM!... WHY, IT CAN'T BE!

IT IS! IT'S **YOU!**

DON'T WORRY SYD, **I'M** THE REAL TOMMY BROWN.

THEN IF YOU'RE TOMMY BROWN, **WHO AM I?**

I THINK I CAN ANSWER THAT!

SHAKIN' STEVENS!

GOSH SHAKEY! I'VE GOT ALL YOUR RECORDS.

EXCUSE ME, BUT ANY TIME YOU'RE READY, PERHAPS WE COULD START THIS CUP FINAL.

CERTAINLY REF. THE LADS ARE RARING TO GO.

THE MATCH KICKS OFF - AND FULCHESTER'S LARGE-BREASTED REDSKIN WINGER IS QUICKLY ON THE BALL...

THAT'S FINE FOOTWORK FROM BROWN FOX!

YES, GOOD INSTANT SKILLS FROM THE REDSKIN WINGER.

SHE'S PASSED ONE DEFENDER!

SHE'S CERTAINLY DOMINATING THE FIELD IN THE KEY AREAS.

AND ANOTHER!

SHE'S ONLY GOT THE KEEPER TO BEAT!

GREAT EFFORT!

YES - BUT IT'S BROUGHT AN EQUALLY FINE SAVE FROM BILLY THOMSON IN THE UNITED GOAL!

WAIT A MINUTE... A FINE SAVE FROM THOMSON IN THE UNITED GOAL!

CORNER TO BARNTON.

NICE WORK BROWN FOX, BUT YOU PLAY FOR FULCHESTER REMEMBER?

BUT BROWN FOX PLAYS FOR UNITED SHE WAS ATTACKING HER OWN GOAL!

YOU'RE ON **OUR SIDE!**

C.D. J.S. G.P.D. D.T. 88

WHAT CAN HAVE GOT INTO THE FULL-BOSOMED REDSKIN WINGER?

WILL HER STRANGE BEHAVIOUR COST UNITED THE CUP?

OR WILL THE FULCHESTER MAN/FISH NUMBER ONE SHIRT SAVE THE DAY?

DON'T MISS THE NEXT ISSUE!

Billy the Fish

FULCHESTER UTD ARE FAVOURITES TO WIN THE CUP FINAL AT WEMBLEY. HOWEVER - THEY SUFFER AN EARLY SETBACK WHEN BROWN FOX, THEIR LARGE-BREASTED CHEROKEE WINGER, FORCES A SAVE FROM HER OWN KEEPER; MAN-cum-FISH BILLY THOMSON.

CD·GPD·JS·ST·'88

WHAT'S THE MATTER BROWN FOX? YOU NEARLY GAVE BARNTON AN EARLY LEAD.

ME HEAP SORRY BILLY, BUT IT'S UM TIME OF MONTH.

WHAT'S WRONG WITH BROWN FOX, BOSS?

WOMEN'S THINGS, SYD. IT'S A GOOD JOB WE'VE GOT A USEFUL SUBSTITUTE ON THE BENCH.

IT LOOKS LIKE P.M.T. HAS GOT THE BETTER OF THE UNFORTUNATE REDSKIN WINGER.

YES, BUT WHO'S THIS, WEARING THE NUMBER TWELVE LABCOAT?

WHY, IT'S FULCHESTER'S "NEW SIGNING", PROFESSOR WOLFGANG SCHNELL BSc, Ph.D, THE MIRACULOUS MIDFIELD MATHEMATICAL MAESTRO!

YES.

YOU SEE, LIKE MATHEMATICS, FOOTBALL IS A SCIENCE AND THE SAME RULES APPLY TO BOTH. IF MY CALCULATIONS ARE CORRECT, THE DYNAMIC FORCES APPLIED SHOULD SEE THE BALL SAFELY IN THE BACK OF THE NET.

AFTER A FEW INITIAL CALCULATIONS, THE PROF IS QUICKLY ON THE BALL...

GOOD "ON THE BALL" MATHEMATICS FROM THE BALDING ACADEMIC.

BARNTON ARE NO MATCH FOR HIS GEOMETRIC WIZARDRY.

BUT, WITH THE GOAL IN HIS SIGHTS...

DÄM UNT BLÄST. ZE BATTERY SHE IS DEAD.

BOO!

CRUMBS! A POWER FAILURE HAS PUT PAID TO THE PROF'S PLAN.

HERE, PROFESSOR SCHNELL B.Sc. Ph.D. USE THIS.

THANK YOU, YOUNG MAN.

HE ONLY HAS TO DIFFERENTIATE THE ANGLE AND THE SHOT'S ON!

GOAL!

WOW! HE EVEN INCORPORATED A FORMULA TO SEND THE KEEPER THE WRONG WAY!

WELL, TOMMY, WE'RE ONE UP WITH ONLY THIRTY SECONDS TO GO

YES AND IF THE SCORE REMAINS THE SAME, YOU'VE GOT TO FANCY US TO WIN.

UNITED NEED ONLY KEEP POSSESSION FOR THE NEXT TEN SECONDS AND THE CUP WILL BE THEIRS.

BUT AT THE OTHER END OF THE FIELD...

PEEP!

WELL REF, WHAT D'YOU RECKON?

PENALTY TO BARNTON

SURELY A QUESTION-MARK MUST HANG OVER THAT DECISION.

THE BARNTON NUMBER NINE PREPARES TO TAKE A PENALTY WITH A DIFFERENCE.....

TOMMY- THERE'S A BOMB ATTACHED TO THE BALL.

YES. AND IF BILLY SUCCEEDS IN SAVING THE KICK, IT WILL MEAN CERTAIN DEATH FOR OUR UNUSUAL "FISH-LIKE" KEEPER.

BILLY THOMSON FACES THE MOST IMPORTANT DECISION OF HIS LIFE!

IS BILLY PREPARED TO LAY DOWN HIS LIFE FOR FULCHESTER UNITED?

DON'T MISS THE FINAL EPISODE OF BILLY the FISH IN THE NEXT ISSUE.!!

Billy the Fish!

LEADING BY A GOAL TO NIL, FULCHESTER UNITED LOOK ALL SET TO WIN THE CUP FINAL UNTIL A LAST MINUTE PENALTY IS AWARDED AGAINST THEM. AND WITH A FORTY POUND BOMB ATTACHED TO THE BALL, ANY ATTEMPT TO SAVE THE KICK WILL MEAN INSTANT DEATH FOR FULCHESTER'S BRILLIANT "FISH-LIKE" GOALKEEPER BILLY THOMSON.

A DEATHLY HUSH DESCENDS ON WEMBLEY STADIUM AS THE KICK IS ABOUT TO BE TAKEN...

BILLY CAN EITHER SAVE HIMSELF - OR SAVE THE BALL... AND DIE!

IT'S A TOUGH DECISION FOR THE YOUNG LAD.

THE BARNTON Nº 9 TAKES THE KICK...

AND WITHOUT HESITATION BILLY THROWS HIS SMALL, FISH-LIKE BODY TOWARDS THE BALL...

BILLY! DON'T BE A HERO!

HE'S SAVED IT!

KA-BOOM!

THE NEXT DAY, IN HOSPITAL...

HOW IS HE DOCTOR? WILL HE BE ALRIGHT?

IT'S LOOKING GRIM. I'M AFRAID HE MAY NOT PULL THROUGH.

IF IT WASN'T FOR BILLY'S BRAVERY, WE WOULDN'T HAVE WON THE CUP!

NOT SO FAST!!

THE CUP FINAL'S NOT OVER YET! BOMBS ARE NOT ALLOWED ON THE FIELD OF PLAY...

THE PENALTY WILL HAVE TO BE RETAKEN!

BUT... WHO'LL PLAY IN GOAL?

I WILL!

BILLY! NO, YOU CAN'T! YOU'RE TOO WEAK!

I MUST. FULCHESTER NEED ME.

A FEW HOURS LATER- BACK AT WEMBLEY STADIUM...

ARE YOU SURE YOU WANT TO GO THROUGH WITH THIS BILLY?

LEAVE IT TO ME, BOSS - I'LL BE OKAY.

AFTER BOMB DISPOSAL EXPERTS CHECK THE BALL FOR BOMBS...

BARNTON PREPARE TO RETAKE THE PENALTY...

HE STRUCK THAT BALL WITH THE POWER OF TEN MEN!

A PILEDRIVER! SURELY NOW ITS ALL OVER BAR THE SHOUTING.

YES.

AS THE BALL HURTLES GOALWARDS, BILLY STRUGGLES UP FROM HIS BED...

...GROAN... I MUST STOP THAT BALL, I MUST.

HE'S TOO WEAK, BOSS. I DON'T THINK HE'S GOING TO MAKE IT.

BUT, AS THE BALL APPROACHES THE LINE...

HE'S SAVED IT!!

INCREDIBLE! HE'S RISEN FROM HIS DEATHBED TO SAVE THE DAY.

PEEP!

THAT'S IT!

THE FINAL WHISTLE!

FULCHESTER HAVE WON THE CUP!!

HOORAY! WE WON THE CUP! WE WON THE CUP!

HOORAY FOR BILLY!

WHERE IS BILLY?

OH NO! BILLY!!

I'M SORRY BOSS... HE'S GONE. THE STRAIN OF THAT LAST SAVE WAS SIMPLY TOO MUCH.

HE MAY BE DEAD BUT HIS MEMORY WILL LIVE ON FOREVER, SYD. WE SHALL NOT SEE HIS LIKE AGAIN. WHEREVER MEN MAY GATHER TO TALK OF FOOTBALL OR FISH, THEY WILL TOAST THE NAME OF BILLY JOHNSON.

THOMSON BOSS.

the end.

Billy the Fish

TWO YEARS HAVE PASSED SINCE THE TRAGIC DEATH OF FISH-LIKE KEEPER BILLY THOMSON, AND FULCHESTER NOW FIND THEMSELVES FLOUNDERING AT THE FOOT OF THE FOURTH DIVISION. THE ONCE CROWDED TERRACES, ONCE ECHOING TO THE SOUNDS OF SUCCESS, ARE NOW BLEAK AND DESERTED....

HOORAY! TWENTY-TWO NIL!

THAT'S 257 GOALS WE'VE CONCEDED IN 14 GAMES, AND WE'VE YET TO SCORE OURSELVES. IT'S NO WONDER THE RESULTS AREN'T GOING OUR WAY.

I KNOW BOSS. THE LADS ARE AS SICK AS PARROTS.

WE'LL NEVER REPLACE BILLY. THE LAD WAS A FOOTBALLING FISH GENIUS.

YES BOSS. BUT PERHAPS IT'S TIME WE TRIED. AFTER ALL, PLAYING WITHOUT A KEEPER HAS LEFT US PRETTY VULNERABLE AT THE BACK.

MMM. MAYBE YOU'RE RIGHT SYD. ANOTHER RESULT LIKE TODAY'S AND OUR HEADS WILL BE ON THE LINE.

YES BOSS. FOOTBALL IS ALL ABOUT WINNING. IT'S RESULTS THAT COUNT. IT'S A DOG-EAT-DOG GAME WITH NO RUNNERS UP.

I'LL ORGANISE SOME TRIALS FOR MONDAY. PERHAPS THERE'S A KEEPER OUT THERE SOMEWHERE CAPABLE OF STEPPING INTO BILLY'S OLD GLOVES.

AND SO...

WANTED
INCREDIBLY TALENTED
GOALKEEPER
TRIALS TO BE HELD
MONDAY at 2 pm
AT
FULCHESTER STADIUM

MONDAY ARRIVES...

WELL SYD. I WONDER IF ANYONE SAW THE POSTER.

I'LL TAKE A LOOK OUTSIDE AND SEE.

CRIKEY! THERE'S A QUEUE BOSS! THERE MUST QUITE LITERALLY BE DOZENS OF THEM OUT THERE!

WELL LET'S SEE WHAT THEY CAN DO!

RIGHT THEN. WHO'S FIRST?

HOW ABOUT ME PARDNER?

I'M TEX TIMPSON. THEY CALL ME THE COWBOY KEEPER.

BANG!

BANG! BANG!

YEE HA!

ONE THE SAMARITANS WATC

OOPS!

NEXT!

AND...

NEXT!

NEXT!

NEXT!

SOME TIME LATER...

NONE OF THIS LOT ARE ANY USE. I GIVE UP.

COME ON BOSS. LET'S HAVE A CUP OF TEA, THEN HAVE ANOTHER LOOK.

OKAY THEN. PASS ME THE FLASK, WILL YOU SYD.

HERE BOSS... OOOPS! TOO HARD!

OH NO! THE FLASK! IT'LL BE BROKEN!

BUT- BEFORE IT CAN HIT THE GROUND..

WELL HELD YOUNG LAD!

THANK-YOU MR BROWN SIR.

YOU KNOW SYD, THAT YOUNG BALL-BOY WILLY THOMSON REMINDS ME OF SOMEONE... BUT I JUST CAN'T THINK WHO.

HMMMM...

HE'S BEEN WITH US FOR TWO YEARS NOW, EVER SINCE HIS FATHER, WHOM NEITHER HE, NOR ANYONE ELSE, EVER KNEW THE IDENTITY OF, WAS TRAGICALLY KILLED.

TO BE CONTINUED...

Billy the Fish

FULCHESTER UNITED, IN THE DOLDRUMS SINCE THE DEATH OF BILLY THOMSON, HAVE BEEN UNSUCCESSFUL IN THEIR ATTEMPTS TO FIND A REPLACEMENT FOR THE LATE 'FISH-LIKE' KEEPER.

WELL SYD, WE'VE DRAWN A BLANK. WE STILL DON'T HAVE A KEEPER.

YES BOSS - AND TIME IS RUNNING OUT - DON'T FORGET IT'S THE FIRST ROUND OF THE F.A. CUP TOMORROW!

YES. ACTUALLY, THEY SHOULD BE MAKING THE DRAW ABOUT NOW.

NON-LEAGUE NO-HOPERS SUDLEY LANE PAPERBOYS ELEVEN, VERSUS FULCHESTER UNITED...

THAT'S JUST THE KIND OF DRAW I WAS HOPING FOR, SYD.

BUT WHAT ARE WE GOING TO DO FOR A KEEPER, BOSS? THE GAME KICKS OFF IN LESS THAN 24 HOURS.

DON'T WORRY SYD. AGAINST A BUNCH OF AMATEURS WE SHOULDN'T NEED ONE!

THE NEXT DAY, FULCHESTER'S TEAM COACH ARRIVES AT SUDLEY LANE...

THAT'S ODD. THERE'S NO SIGN OF A STADIUM, BOSS.

HEY. ARE YOU FULCHESTER UNITED?

YES. WE'RE LOOKING FOR SUDLEY STADIUM.

THIS IS IT. COME ON. LET'S TOSS FOR KICK-OFF.

SORRY I'M LATE LADS. I WAS HAVING ME TEA.

THE FACILITIES LEAVE A LOT TO BE DESIRED, BOSS.

YES, BUT THIS IS FOOTBALL AT ITS GRASS-ROOTS LEVEL, SYD. AND ONCE THAT WHISTLE GOES, IT'S 11 MEN AGAINST 11 MEN. IT'S THE SAME OLD GAME THE WORLD OVER.

HEY MISTER! GIVE US YOUR COAT!

PARDON?

COME ON. WE NEED IT FOR A GOALPOST.

SOON THE GAME GETS UNDERWAY...

BUFC

FULCHESTER MAKE A LIVELY START...

GERROFF IT!

AW! GISSA GO!

OOF!

UM GOAL!

IT'S THERE!

HEY. THAT WAS NEVER IN!

YES IT WAS!

NO IT WASN'T. IT HIT THE POST!

BUT OVER THE POST IS IN!

NO IT ISN'T!

IT WAS NOWHERE NEAR THE POST ANYWAY! IT WAS IN BY MILES!

HEY MISTER! THAT WAS IN, WASN'T IT?

WELL... ERM... IT'S HARD TO SAY...

GET LOST! IT HIT THE POST DIDN'T IT?

ERM...YES...WELL...

SEE. I TOLD YOU IT WASN'T IN. GOALKICK TO US.

UM BAH!

THAT'S A BIT HARSH, BOSS. IT LOOKED LIKE A GOAL TO ME.

YES. BUT AS THERE'S NO REFEREE, THE MAN WITH THE DOG'S DECISION IS FINAL. WE'LL JUST HAVE TO ACCEPT IT.

YOU'RE RIGHT BOSS. IF WE ONCE QUESTION THE MAN WITH THE DOG'S AUTHORITY, WE MAY AS WELL THROW AWAY THE RULE BOOK UPON WHICH THIS GREAT GAME OF OURS HAS BEEN BUILT FOR CENTURIES PAST.

THE GAME RESTARTS WITH A GOALKICK...

CRASH!

OOPS!

HEY MISTER. WILL YOU GET THE BALL BACK FOR US?

30

Billy the Fish

ONCE MIGHTY FULCHESTER UTD, NOW STRUGGLING AT THE FOOT OF THE 4th DIVISION, HAVE BEEN DRAWN AWAY IN THE FIRST ROUND OF THE F.A. CUP TO NON-LEAGUE NO-HOPERS SUDLEY LANE PAPERBOYS.

BUT WITH ONLY SECONDS TO GO, SUDLEY LOOK SET TO GRAB THE WINNER...

THE SUDLEY FORWARD HAS ONLY THE KEEPER TO BEAT!

IF HE KEEPS CALM AND PICKS HIS SPOT, BILLY THE FISH HAS NO CHANCE!

HE MUST SCORE!

OH WELL. IT LOOKS LIKE CURTAINS FOR US, SYD. I CAN'T SEE THE LAD MISSING FROM THAT RANGE.

BUT JUST AS THE YOUNGSTER IS ABOUT TO STRIKE...

BOBBY! YOUR TEA'S READY!

OH NO! HIS MOTHER'S CALL HAS DISTRACTED THIS INEXPERIENCED YOUNG PLAYER!

WHA..?

THE "FISH-LIKE" KEEPER GRABS THE BALL AND PUNTS IT SWIFTLY UPFIELD...

FLAP!

WOW!!!

SUDLEY DON'T APPEAR TO HAVE A KEEPER!

WHAT A GOAL!

THE BOY/FISH MIRACLE HAS SCORED WITH HIS OWN CLEARANCE!

YES - AND IT'LL BE FULCHESTER UNITED WHOSE NAME GOES INTO THE HAT FOR THE SECOND ROUND DRAW.

THAT WAS A FINE BIT OF FOOTWORK FROM THE YOUNG LAD THOMSON.

YES - THE LAD DONE MARVELLOUS SYD.

I THINK OUR GOALKEEPING PROBLEMS ARE SOLVED!!

GREAT GOAL!

YOU WERE SUPPOSED TO BE IN GOAL!

HOORAH FOR BILLY THE FISH!

NO I WASN'T. IT WAS YOUR TURN!

ON THE COACH HOME...

THE F.A. CUP IS THE ICING ON THE CAKE, BUT WE MUSTN'T FORGET OUR BREAD AND BUTTER, EH BOSS?

YES - WE SIMPLY MUST GET A RESULT IN SATURDAY'S BOTTOM-OF-THE-TABLE CLASH WITH GRIMBLEDON OR WE COULD FIND OURSELVES RELEGATED FROM THE FOOTBALL LEAGUE!!!

BUT, AT FULCHESTER STADIUM...

WHAT'S GOING ON HERE? WHY HAVE THE GATES BEEN PADLOCKED?

GONE BUST CLOSED UNTIL NOTI...

I'M THE OFFICIAL RECEIVER. THIS GROUND IS CLOSED. UNLESS FULCHESTER UNITED REPAY DEBTS OF A MILLION POUNDS BY SATURDAY - THE CLUB WILL BE COMPULSORILY WOUND UP!!

TERRIFIC! HOW ARE WE GOING TO GET A RESULT ON SATURDAY IF WE DON'T HAVE A GROUND TO PLAY ON?

WE NEED TO RAISE A MILLION... BUT HOW?!!

THAT EVENING...

THE PLAYERS HAVE HAD UM WHIP-ROUND BOSS, HERE... £16.23

THANKS - BUT IT SIMPLY ISN'T ENOUGH BROWN FOX

I'VE GOT AN IDEA!

YES SHAKEY - WHAT IS IT?

I COULD DO A BENEFIT SHOW WITH ALL THE PROCEEDS GOING TO THE CLUB!

GREAT IDEA!

NEXT DAY...

WE CAN'T MISS THIS!

HEY! SOUNDS GREAT!

GREAT!

FANTASTIC!

WOW! IT'S SHAKEY!

BENEFIT IN AID OF F.U.F.C. SHAKIN' STEVENS

WOW! THIS WILL MAKE FULCHESTER ROCK 'N' ROLL CITY!

YES! I'VE GOT ALL HIS RECORDS.

THAT NIGHT - FULCHESTER TOWN HALL IS PACKED TO CAPACITY WITH THOUSANDS OF SHAKY FANS...

BACKSTAGE...

WELL DONE SHAKEY! IT'S A SELLOUT! NOW IT'S TIME FOR YOU TO GO OUT AND DO YOUR STUFF!

OKAY MR. BROWN.

WE'LL STAY HERE AND COUNT THE TAKINGS!

SOON THE SHOW IS UNDERWAY...

THERE'S AN OLD PI-ANO AND IT'S PLAYIN' HOT BEHIND THE GREEN DOO-OOR!

GREEN DOO-OOR!

HOORAY FOR SHAKY!

SHAKEY IS GREAT!

IT'S A GREAT SHOW BOSS. SHAKEY'S KNOCKING 'EM DEAD. HOW MUCH HAVE WE RAISED ALTOGETHER?

I DON'T KNOW WHAT THEY'RE DOIN' BUT THEY LAUGH A LOT BEHIND THE GREEN DOO-OOR!

A MILLION POUNDS. I COUNTED IT MYSELF. IT'S ON THE TABLE OVER THERE.

OH NO! I DON'T BELIEVE IT! THE MONEY... IT'S GONE!

I WISH THEY'D LET ME IN SO I CAN FIND OUT WHAT'S BEHIND THE GREEN DOO-OOR!

GREEN DOO-OR!

SOMEONE MUST HAVE STOLEN IT!!

WHO HAS STOLEN THE MONEY, AND CAN IT BE RECOVERED IN TIME TO SAVE THE CLUB? IS THIS THE END FOR FULCHESTER, OR WHAT?

Billy the Fish.

FULCHESTER UTD, UNDER THREAT OF INSOLVENCY, HAVE RAISED ENOUGH MONEY TO SAVE THE CLUB WITH A SHAKIN' STEVENS BENEFIT CONCERT. BUT - NO SOONER HAVE THE TAKINGS BEEN COUNTED - A MILLION POUNDS - THAN THE MONEY VANISHES...

YOU'RE ABSOLUTELY SURE IT WAS ON THIS TABLE BOSS?

YES. IT'S DEFINITELY BEEN STOLEN - BUT HOW?

THE ONLY MEANS OF GETTING INTO THE BACKSTAGE AREA IS THROUGH THIS SMALL AIR DUCT.

BUT NO ORDINARY HUMAN BEING COULD POSSIBLY HAVE GOT THROUGH SUCH A NARROW GAP.

NO - BUT PERHAPS HE COULD!

OF COURSE! THE CIRCUS! IT'S ALL BEGINNING TO MAKE SENSE!

THERE'S NO TIME TO LOSE BOSS! WE MUST GET OVER TO THE CIRCUS AND INVESTIGATE!

ERM... HANG ON SYD. ACTUALLY - I THINK IT WAS THIS TABLE.

YES. LOOK.

PHEW! THAT WAS A CLOSE SHAVE BOSS!

THE NEXT DAY - WITH THEIR DEBTS PAID OFF - FULCHESTER PREPARE FOR THEIR VITAL WEEKEND CLASH WITH GRIMBLEDON.

I WANT 110% EFFORT FOR THE FULL 90 MINUTES - BUT AT THE END OF THE DAY I WANT YOU TO GO OUT THERE AND ENJOY YOURSELVES.

TOMMY - THE CHAIRMAN WANTS A WORD

IN THE CHAIRMAN'S OFFICE...

TOMMY - THE FANS WANT SUCCESS. AND I'M PREPARED TO PAY FOR IT. THE MONEY'S ON THE TABLE AND I'M WILLING TO PUT IT WHERE MY MOUTH IS. JUST NAME THE PLAYER, TOMMY - AND YOU'VE GOT HIM.

THE NEXT DAY...

READ ALL ABOUT IT!

Clarion
FULCHESTER
IN £1M +
MYSTERY
BIG STAR
SIGNING
MYSTERY

THAT SATURDAY - FULCHESTER STADIUM IS BUZZING WITH HUSHED ANTICIPATION AS A CAPACITY CROWD AWAITS THE APPEARANCE OF THE NEW MYSTERY SIGNING...

IN THE MANAGER'S OFFICE...

I HOPE I'LL BE ABLE TO LIVE UP TO MY OVER ONE MILLION POUNDS PRICE TAG MR. BROWN.

DON'T WORRY ABOUT THE OVER ONE MILLION POUNDS PRICE - EVEN THOUGH IT IS AN AWFUL LOT OF MONEY.

JUST GO OUT THERE AND ENJOY YOURSELF.

KICK-OFF APPROACHES...

THE PLAYERS ARE COMING ONTO THE PITCH.

I CAN'T SEE THE MYSTERY SIGNING YET

NEITHER CAN I.

HERE HE COMES NOW!

CAN YOU SEE WHO IT IS?

YES... IT'S...

WHY!

I DON'T BELIEVE IT!

IT CAN'T BE... BUT IT IS!

IT'S MICK HUCKNALL OUT OF SIMPLY RED!!

WOW!

WE ALL KNOW WHAT THE LAD CAN DO IN FRONT OF A MICROPHONE.

YES - LET'S SEE IF HE CAN EQUAL IT ON THE FIELD.

WE'LL HAVE TO PULL OUT ALL THE STOPS BOSS. IF WE LOSE TODAY, WE'RE OUT OF THE FOOTBALL LEAGUE.

YES - BUT IF WE CAN WIN BY A CLEAR MARGIN OF 4 GOALS (NOT INCLUDING PENALTIES) WE'LL GO STRAIGHT INTO THE FIRST DIVISION, ON AGGREGATE.

BUT WHAT ABOUT DIVISIONS TWO AND THREE, BOSS?

YOU'RE FORGETTING, SYD - AWAY GOALS COUNT DOUBLE.

SOON THE MATCH GETS UNDERWAY. BILLY THE FISH FEEDS PROFESSOR WOLFGANG SCHNELL B.Sc. PhD. WELL INSIDE HIS OWN HALF.

FINE FIN SKILLS FROM THE PISCINE NUMBER-ONE SHIRT.

A GEOMETRICALLY PERFECT FOOT TRAP BUYS THE PROFESSOR TIME TO MAKE A DEAD BALL CALCULATION.

YES.

ACCURACY TO SIX DECIMAL PLACES!

STRAIGHT TO THE UNSEEN HEAD OF JOHNNY X - FULCHESTER'S INVISIBLE STRIKER

A DEFT TOUCH FINDS THE FEET OF STAR CENTRE FORWARD SHAKIN' STEVENS.

I'VE GOT ALL HIS RECORDS

OH NO!

HE'S FUMBLED IT!

BUT NO! SHAKEY'S SKILFUL FLICK HAS WRONG-FOOTED THE GRIMBLEDON DEFENCE!

YES, AND HE'S PUT FLEETFOOT WINGER BROWN FOX IN THE CLEAR!

SHE BEATS ONE MAN...

AND ANOTHER!

SHE'S NUTMEGGED THE GRIMBLEDON No. 3 TO REACH THE DEAD BALL LINE.

CAN SHE GET THE BALL IN?

YES!

IT LOOKS LIKE A TELLING CROSS!

YES. IT COULD PAY DIVIDENDS IF SOMEONE CAN GET ON THE END OF IT AND DO THE DAMAGE WHERE IT MATTERS - IN THE SIX YARD BOX.

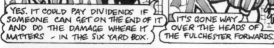

NO... IT'S TOO DEEP.

IT'S GONE WAY OVER THE HEADS OF THE FULCHESTER FORWARDS.

BUT...

WOW!!

BRR

THE LAD HUCKNALL OUT OF SIMPLY RED HAS COME FROM NOWHERE - AND UNLEASHED A FEROCIOUS VOLLEY!!

GOAL!!

FANTASTIC SHOT!

HOORAY FOR MICK OUT OF SIMPLY RED!

AFTER THE RESTART, FULCHESTER QUICKLY HAMMER HOME THE ADVANTAGE WITH ANOTHER GOAL.

A PILEDRIVER FROM THE TRANSPARENT LEFT FOOT OF JOHNNY X!

IT'S THERE!!

AND ANOTHER...

THE FULCHESTER FORWARDS ARE TEARING THE GRIMBLEDON DEFENCE APART LIKE BUTTER!

THREE NIL!

AND ANOTHER...

PROFESSOR WOLFGANG SCHNELL BSc. PhD'S TRIGONOMETRICALLY CALCULATED HEADER PLACES UNITED FIRMLY IN THE DRIVING SEAT.

GREAT GOAL!!

THAT'S FOUR NIL SYD. WE'RE MAKING INROADS ON THE FLANKS AND DOMINATING THE FIELD IN THE KEY AREAS.

ABSOLUTELY BOSS. AND NOW IF WE CAN ONLY MAINTAIN THIS FOUR GOAL MARGIN OVER GRIMBLEDON, IT'LL SEE US SAFELY BACK IN THE FIRST DIVISION, ON AGGREGATE.

UNITED PUSH FORWARD AGAIN FOR A FIFTH GOAL TO PUT THE RESULT BEYOND DOUBT...

IT'S A GOLDEN OPPORTUNITY!

AN OPEN GOAL!

HUCKNALL OUT OF SIMPLY RED MUST SCORE!!

THE KEEPER COMMITTED HIMSELF TOO EARLY!

OOOH! HE'S SKIED IT OVER THE BAR!

HE'S LEFT THE GOALMOUTH COMPLETELY UNGUARDED - THERE'S NO WAY THE FLAME-HAIRED MINSTREL OF SOUL IS GOING TO MISS THIS ONE!

YES.

SECONDS LATER - THE TOUSLE-LOCKED SONGSTER GETS A CHANCE TO REDEEM HIMSELF

A PINPOINT DEFENCE-SPLITTING PASS FROM THE BUXOM SQUAW.

HUCKNALL OUT OF SIMPLY RED ONLY HAS THE KEEPER TO BEAT!

BUT

BOO!

HISS!

WHAT A LOAD OF RUBBISH!

HOOF!

IN A SADLY IRONIC ECHO OF HIS MUSICAL CAREER MICK HUCKNALL OUT OF SIMPLY RED'S PROMISING EARLY SUCCESS HAS BEEN FOLLOWED UP WITH A SERIES OF LACKLUSTRE DISAPPOINTMENTS.

THE FULL-TIME WHISTLE!

PEEP!

FULCHESTER WIN BY A CLEAR FOUR GOALS!

BACK IN DIVISION ONE, IT LOOKS LIKE OUR PROBLEMS ARE OVER EH SYD?

NO BOSS.

I THINK YOU OUGHT TO SEE THIS!

GASP!

I SLEPT WITH TOMMY BROWN! BY PAMELA SLAG

WILL THIS SPELL THE END FOR FULCHESTER? COULD THESE SORDID REVELATIONS IN THE PRESS FORCE TOMMY BROWN'S RESIGNATION?

*

DON'T MISS THE NEXT EPISODE!!

Billy the Fish

FULCHESTER'S RESOUNDING VICTORY OVER GRIMBLEDON HAS SECURED THEM PROMOTION BACK INTO THE 1st DIVISION. BUT - IN THE MIDST OF THE CELEBRATIONS, STEAMY GUTTER PRESS REVELATIONS ABOUT MANAGER TOMMY BROWN'S PRIVATE LIFE LOOK SET TO FORCE HIS RESIGNATION...

IS IT TRUE BOSS? DID YOU SLEEP WITH THIS WOMAN?

OH!! THAT'S OKAY THEN!

YES. I CAN'T DENY IT SYD SEVERAL TIMES - OVER A PERIOD OF YEARS.

BUT IT'S ALRIGHT. SHE'S MY WIFE.

PHEW! THAT WAS A CLOSE SHAVE!

SEVERAL MONTHS LATER...

THE TEAM ARRIVES FOR TRAINING...

DID YOU HAVE A GOOD TIME?

YES. SMASHING.

ME TOO.

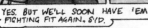

THE LADS ARE LOOKING A BIT OUT OF SHAPE AFTER THE BREAK, TOMMY.

PUFF! PANT!

GASP!

YES. BUT WE'LL SOON HAVE 'EM FIGHTING FIT AGAIN, SYD.

HALF AN HOUR LATER...

OKAY LADS. THAT'S GREAT. TIME FOR A SHOWER.

SHORTLY...

WELL DONE. YOU'VE ALL DONE A GOOD DAY'S WORK TODAY LADS. SEE YOU ALL TOMORROW.

RIGHT YOU ARE BOSS.

EXCEPT YOU BILLY... CAN I SEE YOU IN MY OFFICE FOR A MOMENT?

SO...

I'VE GOT BIG PLANS FOR THIS SEASON, BILLY. I'M BRINGING IN NEW FACES - STRENGTHENING THE SQUAD.

GOOD IDEA BOSS. THE BACK FOUR LEFT ME OVER-EXPOSED ON SEVERAL OCCASIONS LAST SEASON.

...AND CHANCES WENT BEGGING UP FRONT. WE COULD USE A BALL WINNER IN THE MIDDLE OF THE PARK TOO...

WELL ACTUALLY BILLY...

I'M MAKING CHANGES IN YOUR DEPARTMENT.

WHAT??

YES - I'M BUYING A NEW KEEPER!

BUT BOSS, I'VE GIVEN 110% - AND YOU CAN'T ASK FOR ANY MORE THAN THAT.

I'M SORRY BILLY. I'VE GOT BIG PLANS FOR FULCHESTER - AND YOU DON'T FIGURE IN THEM.

I'M LETTING YOU GO, BILLY. I'M GIVING YOU A FREE TRANSFER.

BUT I'VE PLAYED MY HEART OUT FOR THIS CLUB. FULCHESTER UNITED IS MY LIFE!

I'M SORRY BILLY. IT'S FOR THE GOOD OF THE CLUB. I ONLY HOPE THAT WE CAN REMAIN GOOD FRIENDS. I'M SURE YOU UNDERSTAND.

BUT BOSS...

HERE'S A WEEK'S WAGES IN ADVANCE. THIS SECURITY GUARD WILL ESCORT YOU TO THE GATES

NOW GET OUT! AND DON'T EVER SET FOOT IN FULCHESTER STADIUM AGAIN!

B..BUT...

COME ON NOW WE DON'T WANT ANY TROUBLE.

WELL SYD, WE'VE LOST PROBABLY THE GREATEST GOALKEEPER FULCHESTER UNITED HAS EVER HAD. IT'S GOING TO BE IMPOSSIBLE TO REPLACE HIM. BUT WE HAVE TO TRY.

?

THE FANS WILL EXPECT A BIG NAME REPLACEMENT, BOSS. HAVE YOU GOT ANYONE IN MIND?

YES SYD. I'VE BEEN DOING SOME THINKING.

HAVE YOU EVER NOTICED THAT IN THE 100 YEAR HISTORY OF THIS CLUB, NOT A SINGLE NON-JEWISH GOALKEEPER HAS WORN THE FULCHESTER UNITED NUMBER ONE SHIRT?

WELL, I BELIEVE THE TIME HAS COME TO PUT AN END TO THIS RELIGIOUS INTOLERANCE. I AM GOING TO SIGN FULCHESTER'S FIRST CATHOLIC GOALKEEPER!

GREAT IDEA BOSS! YOU'RE RIGHT! WE SHOULD BE BUILDING BRIDGES - NOT WALLS.

WHO WERE YOU THINKING OF?

I'M GOING TO SIGN CARDINAL BASIL HUME - THE LEADER OF THE ROMAN CATHOLIC CHURCH IN BRITAIN.

OPERATOR - GET ME THE VATICAN.

THE NEXT DAY...

READ ALL ABOUT IT!

FULCHESTER SIGN TOP CATHOLIC CLERGY-MAN SHOCK!

A WEEK LATER, UNITED ARE AT HOME TO WALFORD TOWN IN A PRE-SEASON FRIENDLY...

IN THE CHANGING ROOM...

ALRIGHT YOUR HOLINESS. JUST GO OUT THERE AND ENJOY YOURSELF.

ESPIRITU SANCTUM, BOSS. EVEN UNTO THE NINETIETH MINUTE SHALL I GIVETH 110%. MAY THE LORD BE WITH YOU.

AND ALSO WITH YOU, BAZ, YOUR EMINENCE.

Billy the Fish

FIVE HOURS LATER... HOPELESSLY WIDE AGAIN! BOO! WHAT A LOAD OF RUBBISH!

THE SCORE REMAINS 0-0... PHEEEP! THE FULL-TIME WHISTLE!

YES THIS IS A DISTINCTLY LACK-LUSTRE DISPLAY BY THE FULCHESTER FRONT LINE.

THE NEXT DAY IN MANAGER TOMMY BROWN'S OFFICE...

SAY BOSS - THIS IS A NICE RECORD ISN'T IT.

YES. IT'S FANTASTIC! I'M NOT A BIG FAN OF POP MUSIC MYSELF. BUT THIS IS DIFFERENT. I REALLY LIKE IT!

IT'S CALLED "I'LL SAIL THIS SHIP ALONE" AND IT'S THE BRAND NEW POP HIT FROM THE BEAUTIFUL SOUTH, OUT NOW ON GO! DISCS RECORDS.

YES. IT'S AVAILABLE IN SEVEN AND TWELVE INCH VERSIONS AND ALSO AS A CD SINGLE, I HEAR.

BUT NEVER MIND THAT RIGHT NOW, TOMMY, HAVE YOU SEEN TODAY'S NEWSPAPERS?

NOT YET, NO.

BROWN MUST GO! Fulchester Fiasco!

IT'S A BORE DRAW! Fans lose out in 5 hour Snoozathon. Sack Tommy Brown!

THE PRESS ARE ON MY BACK SYD. WE WERE DISAPPOINTING. AND THE BLAME RESTS ULTIMATELY AT MY FEET. MY HEAD'S ON THE LINE..

DON'T WORRY BOSS. IT'LL COME GOOD. AFTER ALL, THE SEASON HASN'T EVEN STARTED YET.

DON'T YOU WORRY SYD, I'M NO QUITTER AND I'M NOT ABOUT TO TURN MY BACK ON FULCHESTER. I'M STAYING.

I'VE GOT A MOUNTAIN TO CLIMB, BUT I'LL SEE THIS JOB THROUGH IF IT'S THE LAST THING I DO.

I'LL DO ANYTHING FOR THIS CLUB, SYD. BUT I'VE JUST ABOUT HAD IT UP TO HERE.

AND NOW IT'S MY WIFE AND KIDS WHO ARE SUFFERING. AND THAT'S A PRICE I'M NOT PREPARED TO PAY. I'M SORRY SYD..

I'M HANGING UP MY COAT. I'M NOT GOING TO TAKE ANY MORE OF THIS HARASSMENT. I'VE HAD ENOUGH.

BUT SURELY BOSS... YOU DON'T MEAN...

YES SYD. I QUIT. I'M RESIGNING AS MANAGER OF FULCHESTER UNITED FOOTBALL CLUB.

GOOD LUCK SYD.

YOU'LL NEED IT.

THAT EVENING IN THE FULCHESTER ARMS...

DID YOU SEE THE MATCH? BORING OR WHAT!? UNITED WERE HOPELESS.

YES. WHAT A FIASCO. IT WAS A DISGRACE.

WHAT FULCHESTER NEEDS IS A SOLID TARGET MAN IN THE 18 YARD BOX. SOMEONE WHO CAN PUT THE BALL IN THE BACK OF THE NET AT THE END OF THE DAY.

PARDON? WHAT DO YOU KNOW ABOUT FOOTBALL? YOU'RE JUST AN OVERWEIGHT, "FISH-LIKE" PUB LANDLORD WHO DRINKS TOO MUCH!

YEAH. KEEP YOUR COMMENTS TO YOURSELF.

HA HA HA HA!

HO HO HO HO!

SNIFF!

IF ONLY THEY KNEW. YESTERDAY I HAD THE WORLD AT MY FEET. IT WAS IN THE PALM OF MY HAND. I USED TO BE SOMEBODY. I USED TO BE A CONTENDER...

AND NOW I'M JUST A USELESS DRUNKEN NOBODY. WHAT I WOULDN'T GIVE TO GET BACK INTO FOOTBALL...

HELLO. WHAT'S THIS?...

TOMMY RESIGNS

GOSH! TOMMY BROWN HAS QUIT!

THAT MEANS THE FULCHESTER UNITED HOT-SEAT IS UP FOR GRABS!

HELLO? OPERATOR?

GET ME FULCHESTER UNITED. I WANT TO SPEAK TO THE CHAIRMAN - RICK SPANGLE.

HELLO. MR. SPANGLE? THIS IS BILLY "THE FISH" THOMSON...

I WANT TO BE THE NEXT MANAGER OF FULCHESTER UNITED FOOTBALL CLUB!

WHAT'S TO BECOME OF FULCHESTER NOW THAT TOMMY BROWN HAS HUNG UP HIS COAT?

WILL BILLY THE FISH TAKE OVER THE UNITED HELM?

WILL "I'LL SAIL THIS SHIP ALONE", THE FABULOUS NEW SINGLE BY THE BEAUTIFUL SOUTH MAKE IT TO THE TOP OF THE XMAS POP CHARTS?*

DON'T MISS THE NEXT EPISODE!

*HISTORICAL NOTE: LIKE ARSE IT DID.

38

Billy the Fish

39

IN THE WAKE OF TOMMY BROWN'S SHOCK RESIGNATION AS MANAGER OF FULCHESTER UNITED, DEPOSED FORMER GOALKEEPER BILLY 'THE FISH' THOMSON, NOW ALCOHOLIC LANDLORD OF THE FULCHESTER TAVERN, HAS TELEPHONED CHAIRMAN RICK SPANGLE TO APPLY FOR THE VACANT POST...

HELLO?

YES?

MR. SPANGLE? IT'S ME, BILLY THE FISH, SACKED GOALKEEPER, NOW LANDLORD OF THE FULCHESTER ARMS.

I HEREBY APPLY FOR THE POSITION OF MANAGER OF FULCHESTER UNITED FOOTBALL CLUB!

SORRY PAL. YOU'VE GOT THE WRONG NUMBER.

BILLY DIALS AGAIN...

HELLO - IS THAT FULCHESTER UNITED FOOTBALL CLUB?

YES. CHAIRMAN RICK SPANGLE SPEAKING.

THIS IS BILLY 'THE FISH' THOMSON SPEAKING. I WANT THE MANAGER'S JOB, MR. SPANGLE. I'M THE MAN - FISH FOR YOU!

WHY - I'M SORRY BILLY. THAT VACANCY HAS JUST BEEN FILLED.

HAVEN'T YOU HEARD? WE APPOINTED A NEW MANAGER ONLY THIS AFTERNOON. IN FACT, HE'S WITH ME NOW.

TOMMY BROWN HAS SUCCESSFULLY RE-APPLIED FOR HIS OLD JOB... AND HE'S GOT BIG PLANS FOR FULCHESTER UNITED.

HELLO? BILLY? I'VE GOT BIG PLANS FOR FULCHESTER UNITED - AND I WANT YOU TO BE A PART OF THEM.

WE WANT YOU BACK, BILLY. LET'S PUT THE PAST BEHIND US. IT'S HISTORY. ALL THAT MATTERS NOW IS THE FUTURE. AND YOUR FUTURE IS HERE AT FULCHESTER ROAD.

NAME YOUR PRICE, BILLY. WE NEED YOU BACK. YOU CAN WRITE YOUR OWN PAY CHEQUE.

THE MONEY'S ON THE TABLE TOMMY. IT'S ALWAYS BEEN AVAILABLE. YOU KNOW THAT.

THIS IS A BIG DECISION TOMMY. I'VE BEEN OUT OF FOOTBALL A LONG TIME. I NEED BREATHING SPACE. I'LL HAVE TO TALK IT OVER WITH MY WIFE AND KIDS.

YOU CAN HAVE ALL THE TIME YOU NEED, BILLY. DON'T RUSH YOUR DECISION.

BUT I MUST HAVE AN ANSWER BY 9 O'CLOCK TOMORROW MORNING.

THAT EVENING, BILLY ARRIVES HOME...

DON'T DO IT BILLY. THINK OF THE KIDS. MONEY ISN'T EVERYTHING. YOU'VE GOT A GOOD JOB AT THE PUB. DON'T GO BACK, BILLY.

YOU'RE RIGHT DARLING. I WON'T LET FOOTBALL COME BETWEEN US AGAIN. IF THE CHOICE IS BETWEEN FOOTBALL AND MY FAMILY - THERE'S ONLY ONE DECISION I CAN MAKE.

THE NEXT MORNING AT FULCHESTER STADIUM...

IT'S GREAT TO SEE YOU BILLY. I KNEW YOU'D COME BACK TO US!

YES. WELCOME BACK BILLY!

I'M SORRY TOMMY. I'M NOT STOPPING. I CAME TO SAY GOODBYE.

B-BUT... WHY?

YOU KNOW THAT FOOTBALL IS THE MOST IMPORTANT THING IN MY LIFE, TOMMY. BUT MY FAMILY COMES FIRST. I'VE GOT TO THINK OF THEM.

I'M SORRY TOMMY. AS LONG AS I'VE GOT A WIFE AND KIDS, FOOTBALL WILL ALWAYS TAKE SECOND PLACE IN MY LIFE.

EXCUSE ME, MR. THE FISH.

I'M AFRAID I'VE GOT SOME BAD NEWS FOR YOU. THERE'S BEEN A TERRIBLE ACCIDENT. YOUR WIFE AND CHILDREN ARE ALL DEAD.

BILLY. I'M SO TERRIBLY SORRY...

YES. IF THERE'S ANYTHING I CAN DO...

YES. SNIFF... THERE IS... SNIFF...

GET ME MY BOOTS! WE'VE GOT A FOOTBALL MATCH TO PLAY!

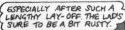

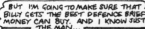

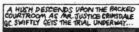

Billy the Fish.

DUE TO A LOOPHOLE IN THE LAW, YOUNG BILLY THOMSON IS ABOUT TO BE HANGED FOR A CRIME THAT DID NOT TAKE PLACE.

'MOREOVER – AS FULCHESTER'S OFFICIAL HANGMAN– UNITED COACH SYD PRESTON IS DUE TO CARRY OUT THE SENTENCE!

THE NEXT DAY BILLY'S FULCHESTER TEAM-MATES VISIT HIM ON DEATH ROW

I'M SORRY IT HAD TO END THIS WAY BILLY.

IS THERE NOTHING YOU CAN DO, BOSS?

I ONLY WISH THERE WAS.

ZERE EES VON SING ZAT JUST MIGHT VORK BOSS.

WHAT'S THAT PROFESSOR?

ZISS IS EIN TIME MACHINE. HOPEFULLY VEN I PULL ZE LEVER VEE VILL BE TRANSPORTED BACK IN TIME!

AND OUT OF THIS JAM! QUICK! GIVE IT A PULL PROFESSOR!

VERY VELL. HERE GOES...

WHOOSH!

I ONLY HOPE IT WORKS.

ZERE EES VON SING ZAT JUST MIGHT VORK BOSS.

WHAT'S THAT PROFESSOR?

ZISS IS EIN TIME MACHINE...

ER., PERHAPS YOU COULD TRY PULLING IT A LITTLE BIT FURTHER THIS TIME.

AH YES.

WHOOSH!

CRUMBS- NOW WE'VE GONE BACK TO CAVE-MAN DAYS!

TRY IT AGAIN PROFESSOR.

WHOOSH!

PHEW! THAT'S BETTER. WE HAVE ARRIVED BACK IN THE DYING SECONDS OF OUR FIRST MATCH OF THE SEASON – AT HOME TO ARCH-RIVALS GRIMTHORPE.

THANK GOODNESS FOR THAT.

BUT... QUICKLY BILLY! GRIMTHORPE ARE ABOUT TO SCORE!

OH NO!

JUST LEAVE IT TO ME!

BILLY WASTES NO TIME...

GOSH. WHERE DID HE COME FROM?

IT'S AS IF THE LAD THOMSON HAS BEEN SOMEHOW WHISKED BACK FROM THE FUTURE IN ORDER TO SAVE THE DAY, OR SOMETHING.

WOW! AND WHAT A SAVE! HE STRUCK THAT BALL WITH ALL THE FORCE OF A TEN TON TRUCK!

YES.

GNN!

HOORAY FOR BILLY THE FISH!

WITH THE SCORE STILL AT 0-0, ONE GOAL WOULD BE ENOUGH TO SECURE US A RESULT BOSS.

YES SYD. PROVIDING OF COURSE IT'S US THAT SCORES THAT GOAL.

THERE'S ONLY SECONDS LEFT TO PLAY NOW.

YES. BUT THAT'S A LIKELY LOOKING CROSS DEEP INTO THE 18 YARD BOX FROM THE FLEETFOOT REDSKIN BROWN FOX.

BLIND 64-YEAR OLD VETERAN REX FINDLAY AND HIS GUIDE DOG SHEP ARE QUICKLY ON THE BALL.

WHERE IS IT, SHEP?

WOOF! WOOF!

WOOF!

WHAT A FANTASTIC BICYCLE KICK!

BOOT!

WOOF!

YES, THE OLD-TIMER'S EYES MAY HAVE DESERTED HIM – BUT HIS RIGHT FOOT HAS LOST NONE OF ITS APPETITE FOR THE GAME.

BAH!

GOAL!

IT PROVES TO BE THE FINAL KICK OF THE GAME

THE FULL-TIME WHISTLE!

PEEP!

VICTORY FOR UNITED!

IN THE CHANGING ROOMS...

WELL DONE LADS. WE WENT OUT THERE TO PLAY FOOTBALL. WE KEPT IT TIGHT AT THE BACK AND TOOK THE GAME TO THEM IN THE FIRST PERIOD. AT THE END OF NINETY MINUTES WE GAVE 110% AND I THINK WE DESERVED TO COME AWAY WITH A RESULT AT THE END OF THE DAY.

BUT SUDDENLY... EXCUSE ME. YOU'LL ALL HAVE TO GET OUT. THESE DRESSING ROOMS ARE ABOUT TO BE DEMOLISHED.

DEMOLISHED? ON WHO'S AUTHORITY?

ON MY AUTHORITY, MR. BROWN!

AND JUST WHO THE HELL ARE YOU?

I'M MILLIONAIRE DEVELOPER WINYARD HALL –THE MAN BEHIND THE FULCHESTER SHOPPING PRECINCT...

...AND NOW I'M A DIRECTOR OF FULCHESTER UNITED!

I'VE GOT BIG PLANS FOR THE CLUB. I'M GOING TO MAKE THIS GROUND INTO EUROPE'S LARGEST INDOOR MULTI-COMPLEX AIR-CONDITIONED SHOPPING AND LEISURE CENTRE

AND I WILL BRING JOBS TO THE AREA AND PROSPERITY TO MYSELF AND MY IMMEDIATE RELATIVES.

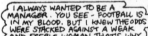

Billy the Fish

FULCHESTER UNITED HAVE BEEN ROCKED BY MANAGER TOMMY BROWN'S SHOCK REVELATION THAT HE IS A WOMAN, SAMANTHA, PREGNANT WITH BILLY "THE FISH" THOMSON'S LOVE CHILD...

NOW READ ON...

THE NEXT DAY, THE MANAGERESS IS LATE FOR TRAINING...

I WONDER WHERE SAMANTHA IS.

YES. SHE'S BRINGING A CAKE RECIPE FOR MY WIFE TODAY.

SUDDENLY, A STRANGER APPEARS...

HELLO...

WHO'S THIS?

YOU DON'T KNOW ME, BUT SAMANTHA BROWN ASKED ME TO DELIVER A MESSAGE.

SHE HAS GONE TO BRAZIL FOR EVER. I AM HER TWIN BROTHER THOMAS, AND I WILL BE TAKING OVER AS MANAGER OF FULCHESTER UNITED.

FAIR ENOUGH. YOU'RE THE BOSS NOW, THOMAS.

JUST CALL ME TOMMY, SYD.

GATHER ROUND LADS. WE'VE GOT A TOUGH GAME ON SATURDAY, AGAINST ROSSDALE ROVERS.

BUT ROSSDALE HAVEN'T WON A MATCH IN EIGHT YEARS!

YES. THEY'RE BOTTOM OF THE LEAGUE AREN'T THEY?

YES. BUT THEY'VE JUST SIGNED STUMPY ARGENTINIAN CHEAT DIEGO MARADONA FOR 10 MILLION POUNDS. HE COULD PROVE QUITE A HANDFUL ON SATURDAY.

GOOD THINKING BOSS.

WE'VE GOT TO KEEP IT TIGHT AT THE BACK, PICK UP THE SPARE MAN, USE THE WIDTH OF THE PARK AND LET THE BALL DO THE WORK.

HOPEFULLY, AT THE END OF THE NINETY MINUTES WE'LL COME AWAY WITH SOME SORT OF RESULT.

SATURDAY ARRIVES - AND A CAPACITY CROWD CRAMS INTO FULCHESTER STADIUM TO WATCH THE FOUR FOOT ARGENTINIAN ACE'S DEBUT FOR ROSSDALE...

MARADONA KICKS OFF FOR ROSSDALE...

PHEEP!

HANDBALL! SURELY!

THE REFEREE MUST BE BLIND!

FREE KICK TO ROSSDALE!

PHEEP!

THE REF'S SHOWING ONE OF THE UNITED PLAYERS THE YELLOW CARD!

CRUMBS!

BUT REF! I NEVER TOUCHED HIM!

A POTENTIALLY DANGEROUS SITUATION EH, BOSS?

YES SYD.

THE ROSSDALE FORWARDS COULD PRODUCE SOMETHING FROM THERE. BILLY THE FISH COULD BE CALLED UPON TO PROVE HIS WORTH!

THE FREE KICK IS TAKEN...

S GO! DISCS GO!

IT'S A CURLING, DIPPING CROSS, AIMED AT THE FAR POST.

YES, BUT AT FOUR FOOT TWO, MARADONA WON'T BE ABLE TO GET ANYWHERE NEAR IT.

BILLY'S GOT THAT ONE SAFELY COVERED.

BUT—

GOT

BUT NO! BILLY'S BEEN BEATEN!

LOB

GOAL TO ROSSDALE!

?

SHADES OF HANDBALL, EH BOSS?

IT CERTAINLY LOOKED THAT WAY FROM WHERE I'M SITTING. BUT THE REFEREE WAS WELL POSITIONED TO JUDGE FOR HIMSELF - AND HIS DECISION IS FINAL.

FULCHESTER REPLY WITH A QUICK BREAK...

BROWN FOX HAS A CLEAR RUN AT THE ROSSDALE GOAL!

YES!

UM FOUL!

FREE KICK SURELY!

TRIP!

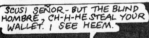

Billy the Fish

DESPITE BEING BORN HALF MAN/HALF FISH, BILLY THOMSON HAS MADE THE FULCHESTER UTD No. 1 SHIRT HIS OWN...

BUT NOW HE HAS TURNED HIS BACK ON THE CLUB IN ORDER TO GO TO BED WITH KYLIE MINOGUE IN HER AUSTRALIAN LOVE NEST.

THE NEXT DAY, BILLY ARRIVES IN AUSTRALIA... I CAN'T BELIEVE IT. IT'S ONLY A MATTER OF SECONDS TILL I GO TO BED WITH KYLIE MINOGUE. I'M QUIVERING ALL OVER.

HELLO. KYLIE MINOGUE SPEAKING. WHO IS IT? IT'S ME. BILLY.

I'M HERE TO GO TO BED WITH YOU, AS PER OUR TELEPHONE CONVERSATION. OOH BILLY! I'LL BE RIGHT DOWN!

KYLIE! STRUTH! WHO ARE YOU?

WHY, I'M BILLY THOMSON. YOU WANTED TO GO TO BED WITH ME, REMEMBER? BILLY THOMSON?

I WANTED TO GO TO BED WITH BILLY IDOL. I MUST HAVE GOT THE WRONG NUMBER. OH NO!

SO... THERE'S NO CHANCE OF YOU GOING TO BED WITH ME AFTER ALL? HA! YOU SHOULD BE SO LUCKY. I DON'T EVEN SLIGHTLY FANCY YOU. YOU'RE A FISH.

SLAM! SNIFF

MEANWHILE, ON THE OTHER SIDE OF THE WORLD, AT FULCHESTER STADIUM, THE SECOND HALF GETS UNDERWAY... WITHOUT BILLY. PHEEP!

AND THE EMPTY FULCHESTER GOALMOUTH IS SOON UNDER ATTACK. THIS BREAK COULD BE DANGEROUS! YES. THIS LAD LOOKS A BIT TASTY.

HAVING NO KEEPER LEAVES OUR GOAL VULNERABLE TO ATTACK. YES. WE'RE LOOKING A BIT THIN IN THE 6-YARD BOX.

AN OPEN GOAL! HE CANNOT MISS! TWO-NIL TO ROSSDALE SURELY! BUT WHAT'S THAT IN THE SKY - ABOVE OUR HEADS?

WHY! IT CAN'T BE! IT IS!

IT'S BILLY THE FISH!

AND HE'S JUST IN TIME TO SAVE THE DAY! HOORAH!!

A REMARKABLE SAVE, EH BOSS. THE LAD TRAVELLED ALL OF 12,000 MILES, THEN PARACHUTED OUT OF A JUMBO JET TO PUSH THAT ONE ROUND THE POST! YES. LUCKY FOR US THAT THE TIME DIFFERENCE BETWEEN AUSTRALIA AND BRITAIN ENABLED BILLY TO ARRIVE BACK WITHIN ONLY MINUTES OF LEAVING.

FORTY MINUTES LATER AND THE SCORE REMAINS 1-0 TO ROSSDALE... THE GAME APPEARS TO BE SLIPPING OUT OF FULCHESTER'S GRASP. I WONDER WHETHER TOMMY BROWN HAS AN ACE LEFT UP HIS SLEEVE... YES. A STRANGE NEW SIGNING PERHAPS. SOMEONE THAT HE HAS OMITTED TO MENTION SO FAR.

TIME TO INTRODUCE A FRESH PAIR OF LEGS, EH BOSS? YES, SYD... FOUR LEGS ACTUALLY!

BUT BOSS - WE'VE ONLY GOT ONE SUBSTITUTE LEFT... HE'S UNDER THAT TARPAULIN OVER THERE. YES SYD. ONE SUBSTITUTE, FOUR LEGS!

I'D LIKE YOU TO MEET MY NEW SIGNING... ...WING AND WONG, THE WANG TWINS' INCREDIBLE FOOTBALLING SIAMESE TWINS JOINED AT THE HIP SINCE THE AGE OF TWO.

THE SUBSTITUTION IS MADE...

THE 4-LEGGED TWINS IMMEDIATELY BEGIN TO MAKE THEIR MARK... CRUMBS! LOOK AT THOSE ORIENTAL MARVELS MOVE!

YES. THEY'RE LITERALLY RUNNING RINGS ROUND ROSSDALE'S DEFENCE. BLOUWN FOX - YOU HAVE BALL.

IS THIS THE END FOR FULCHESTER? IS EVERYONE GOING TO PRISON? DON'T MISS THE NEXT EPISODE - BROUGHT TO YOU BY GO! DISCS PURVEYORS OF FINE QUALITY 'POP' AND 'BEAT' MUSIC TO TODAY'S YOUNGER GENERATION.